LOW-FAT VEGETARIAN COOKBOOK

From the Editors of Sunset Books

Sunset Publishing Corporation
Menlo Park, CA

President & Publisher:
Susan J. Maruyama

Director, Finance & Business Affairs:
Gary Loebner

Director, Sales & Marketing:
Richard A. Smeby

Marketing & Creative Services Manager:
Guy C. Joy

Production Director:
Lory Day

Director, New Business:
Kenneth Winchester

Editorial Director:
Bob Doyle

**EDITORIAL STAFF FOR LOW-FAT
VEGETARIAN COOKBOOK**

Coordinating Editor:
Linda J. Selden

Research & Text:
Karyn I. Lipman

Copy Editor:
Rebecca LaBrum

Contributing Editor:
Sue Brownlee

Design:
Susan Sempere

Illustrations:
Dick Cole

Dietary Consultant:
Patricia Kearney, R.D.
Stanford University Hospital

Photo Stylist:
Sandra Griswold

Food Stylist:
Heidi Gintner

Assistant Food & Photo Stylist:
Elizabeth C. Davis

Photographer:
Allan Rosenberg

Associate Photographer:
Allen V. Lott

Production Coordinator:
Patricia S. Williams

SUNSET PUBLISHING CORPORATION

Chairman:
Jim Nelson

President/Chief Executive Officer:
Robin Wolaner

Chief Financial Officer:
James E. Mitchell

Publisher
Stephen J. Seabolt

Circulation Director:
Robert I. Gursha

Vice President, Manufacturing:
Lorinda B. Reichert

Editor, Sunset Magazine:
William R. Marken

Senior Editor, Food & Entertaining:
Jerry Anne Di Vecchio

First printing September 1995
Copyright © 1995 Sunset Publishing Corporation,
Menlo Park, CA 94025.
First edition. All rights reserved, including the right of
reproduction in whole or in part in any form.
ISBN 0-376-02484-4 Library of Congress
Catalog Card Number: 95-069112.
Printed in the United States

Meatless Meals the Low-fat Way

For lean, flavorful meatless dishes inspired by cuisines from around the world, turn to our new Low-fat Vegetarian Cookbook. Each of the five chapters highlights foods basic to a lacto-ovo vegetarian diet—wholesome fresh produce, satisfying pastas, hearty whole grains, legumes in variety, and eggs and cheese. And every chapter is filled with exciting ideas. Whether you're new to vegetarian cooking or simply want to expand your recipe collection with leaner choices, you'll savor such selections as Broccoli-Cornmeal Kuchen (page 18), Oven-baked Mediterranean Orzo (page 26), Fruited Basmati Pilaf (page 40), Mushroom & White Bean Pizza (page 71), and Indian-spiced Scrambled Eggs (page 87).

✳

Our recipes conform to the American Heart Association's recommendations for fat intake; in each, fat provides no more than 30% of the total calories. Every recipe is accompanied by a nutritional analysis (see page 5) prepared by Hill Nutrition Associates, Inc., of Florida. Starting with this book, the analysis has been expanded to include grams of fiber and milligrams of calcium and iron. We are grateful to Lynne Hill, R.D., for her advice and expertise.

✳

For each recipe, we provide preparation and cooking times. Keep in mind that these times are approximate and will vary depending on your expertise in the kitchen and on the cooking equipment you use.

✳

The recipes in this book were developed in the Sunset test kitchens. If you have comments or suggestions, please let us hear from you. Write to us at:

**Sunset Books/Cookbook Editorial
80 Willow Road
Menlo Park, CA 94025**

If you would like to order additional copies of any of our books, call us at 1 (800) 634-3095 or check with your local bookstore.

✳

Front cover: Wheat Germ Burgers (page 50). Design by Susan Bryant. Photography by Allan Rosenberg. Photo styling by Sandra Griswold. Food Styling by Heidi Gintner.

Contents

Quinoa Risotto
(recipe on page 45)

SPECIAL FEATURES

Introduction

✳

In home kitchens and restaurants alike, meatless eating is on the rise. Why? Great flavor and good nutrition are two compelling reasons. The foods at the heart of a vegetarian diet—fresh fruits and vegetables, pastas, satisfying legumes and whole grains—are both delicious and naturally wholesome. The variety in today's markets keeps meatless cooking exciting, too: each week seems to bring new and improved kinds of produce and a greater assortment of breads, beans, and grains. And while a no-meat diet is not automatically lean, it's easy to create low-fat vegetarian meals. All the tempting recipes in this book conform to the American Heart Association's recommendations for fat intake, deriving no more than 30% of their calories from fat.

The dishes you'll find in the following pages are primarily intended for lacto-ovo vegetarians, who avoid meat, poultry, and fish entirely but do eat dairy products and eggs. In each chapter, though, we've included a few recipes for "almost vegetarians": those who follow a vegetarian diet much of the time, but don't completely exclude meat from their meals.

Some of these recipes contain only enough meat for flavoring: in Autumn Harvest Gratin (page 21), for example, crisp-fried prosciutto lends just a hint of smokiness to a sturdy casserole of sweet potatoes and tender apples. Other "almost vegetarian" choices offer slightly heartier helpings of meat, fish, or poultry. In our Light Cassoulet (page 77), for instance, chicken breast and turkey kielbasa are important ingredients, weighing in at about 4 ounces per serving—but that amount is still significantly less than what you'd find in a classic French cassoulet.

Getting enough protein

✳

Those who are new to vegetarian cooking and eating often wonder if plant foods alone can provide enough protein for a healthful diet. The answer is yes, provided that your meals contain a good variety of whole grains, legumes, and vegetables. To understand why variety is so crucial, you need to know a little about complete versus incomplete protein.

When we say a protein is *complete*, we mean it contains all the essential amino acids (those our bodies cannot produce on their own) in just the proportions our bodies need. Proteins from animal sources, such as milk, eggs, cheese, and meat, are complete.

Proteins from plant sources, however, are almost all *incomplete*: they are lacking or low in one or more essential amino acids. (The exceptions to this rule are soybeans and foods made from them, such as tofu and tempeh; they provide virtually complete protein.) As far as our bodies are concerned, this amino-acid deficiency limits the usability of the entire protein.

The way to solve the incomplete-protein problem is through *protein complementing*: pairing a food that's devoid of or low in certain amino acids with another that contains those acids. Any animal-source protein will complete a plant-source protein, so lacto-ovo vegetarians and "almost vegetarians" can create dishes with high-quality protein simply by adding modest amounts of dairy products, eggs, or meat to an all-vegetable recipe. But protein can be completed by combining plant sources, too: legumes with grains, nuts with legumes, and so on. Many such partnerships are familiar to us from classic dishes such as beans and rice, tortillas and beans, even peanut butter on whole wheat bread.

Throughout this book, you'll find numerous examples of protein complementing. Green & Brown Rice (page 44) pairs brown rice with split peas; Baked Quesadillas (page 81) feature flour tortillas filled with black beans. And for a sophisticated version of PBJ on whole wheat, try our Wheat Berry Satay Salad (page 49): chewy wheat kernels tossed with a spicy dressing based on peanut butter and fruit jam.

When you choose your protein sources for the day's meals, concentrate on combinations that yield high-quality protein without too much fat. By selecting from a wide variety of lean foods and eating them in sensible quantities, you're likely to consume adequate amounts of protein and all other basic nutrients. The main dishes in this book all provide at least 14 grams of protein per serving—the minimum amount you should aim for at each main meal, assuming you're also getting some protein by snacking wisely a few times a day and/or drinking nonfat milk with your meals.

Cutting fat

Like any other kind of low-fat cooking, low-fat vegetarian cuisine depends on low-fat ingredients, lively seasonings, and lean cooking techniques.

Baking, broiling, and steaming are the standard low-fat cooking methods, of course, but many of our recipes feature what we call "braise-deglazing"—really a lean version of pan-frying—to develop a flavorful base of cooked onions or other vegetables for curries, stews, and other dishes. To braise-deglaze, you omit all or almost all of the fat you'd typically use for sautéing, instead adding a little water or broth to the vegetables you want to cook. Stir the mixture over medium-high heat until the vegetables begin to brown and the liquid is gone; then stir in a bit more liquid and repeat the process. You'll find that vegetables browned in this way have every bit as much deep, rich flavor as those sautéed in butter.

Among ingredients, you'll find countless streamlined choices. When buying dairy products such as milk, yogurt, cottage cheese, and sour cream, opt for the nonfat, low-fat, and reduced-fat products so readily available today. Among cheeses, select reduced-fat types or use modest quantities of whole-milk varieties such as feta, blue, and Parmesan. Remember: the more robust the cheese, the more significant the contribution even a small amount will make to a recipe's flavor.

When you're cooking with eggs, use fewer whole eggs and more egg whites. A glance through our chapter of egg and cheese dishes (pages 79–93) will give you numerous examples of this tactic.

One easy way to cut a recipe's percentage of calories from fat is to include a healthy helping of pasta, rice, or legumes. Mild-flavored and rich in complex carbohydrates, these filling foods take well to a variety of sauces and spices.

To make up for the flavor traditionally contributed by fat, turn to extra seasonings. Herbs and spices, zesty vinegars, and intensely flavored condiments all add excitement—but little or no fat—to lean dishes.

Fat contributes to texture, too. To restore the moisture and velvety "mouth feel" you often lose when you trim fat from your recipes, try replacing some of the fat in baked goods with applesauce, mashed bananas, or other fruit purées, or with puréed cottage cheese. The tender pastry for our Chili Pot Pie (page 63), for example, is made with applesauce and cottage cheese. Be aware that, in pastries and other baked goods, there's no set formula for replacing fat with fruit purées. You might start by substituting all the fat in the original recipe with half that quantity of fruit purée. If the results are too dense, dry, or chewy, add back the fat, a tablespoon at a time, until you're pleased with the texture.

Canned cream-style corn, whirled until smooth in the blender or food processor, makes a great thickener for savory sauces, lending the silky texture usually provided by butter, egg yolks, or whipping cream. If you like, play up the corn flavor by adding corn kernels to the dish as well, as in Southwestern Fettuccine (page 24) and Corn Custard (page 90).

If you're looking to cut sodium as well as fat, choose reduced-sodium condiments and no-salt-added canned vegetables. If you have the time, you might also want to prepare your own vegetable broth from scratch, since the canned variety—though it yields excellent results in our recipes—is fairly high in sodium.

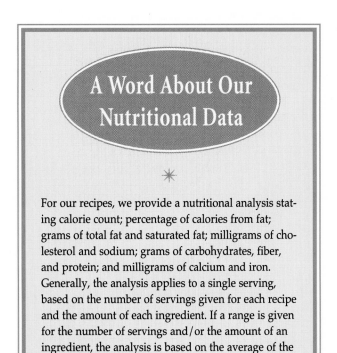

A Word About Our Nutritional Data

For our recipes, we provide a nutritional analysis stating calorie count; percentage of calories from fat; grams of total fat and saturated fat; milligrams of cholesterol and sodium; grams of carbohydrates, fiber, and protein; and milligrams of calcium and iron. Generally, the analysis applies to a single serving, based on the number of servings given for each recipe and the amount of each ingredient. If a range is given for the number of servings and/or the amount of an ingredient, the analysis is based on the average of the figures given.

The nutritional analysis does not include optional ingredients or those for which no specific amount is stated. If an ingredient is listed with a substitution, the information was calculated using the first choice.

Red Slaw
(recipe on page 8)

ALL VEGETABLES

✳

*B*right, flavorful vegetables are the stars in this chapter. Sometimes a single kind plays the main role, as in Crustless Spinach Pie and Broccoli-Cornmeal Kuchen. More often, though, you'll find tempting combinations, as in Potato Curry—featuring green peas, broccoli, and both russet and sweet potatoes—and Roasted Vegetable Pizzettes. And many of our offerings are innovative ones: hearty lasagne layered with sliced eggplant and zucchini instead of noodles, broccoli burgers served with homemade red onion relish, even a crisp pizza with an herb-seasoned crust made from shredded carrots and zucchini.

✳

Red Slaw *(Pictured on page 6)*

1 medium-size head red cabbage (about 2 lbs./905 g)

3 tablespoons (45 ml) *each* balsamic vinegar and salad oil

2 cans (about 15 oz./425 g *each*) red kidney beans, drained and rinsed

1 can (about 15 oz./425 g) pickled beets, drained and coarsely chopped

2 tablespoons finely chopped crystallized ginger

2½ cups (370 g) pitted sweet cherries, fresh or thawed frozen

⅓ to ½ cup (35 to 50 g) thinly sliced green onions

4 whole green onions, ends trimmed (optional)

Salt and pepper

Crystallized ginger, pickled beets, and cherries add spicy and sweet flavors to this vibrant main-dish salad of red cabbage and kidney beans. Try it with warm buttermilk biscuits.

Preparation time: 15 minutes

1 Remove 4 to 8 large outer cabbage leaves and set aside. Then core cabbage and finely shred enough of it to make 5 cups (350 g); set aside. Reserve any remaining cabbage for other uses.

2 In a large bowl, beat vinegar and oil until blended. Stir in beans, beets, and ginger. Gently mix in shredded cabbage and cherries. (At this point, you may cover and refrigerate slaw and whole cabbage leaves separately for up to 4 hours.)

3 To serve, stir sliced onions into slaw. Arrange 1 or 2 of the whole cabbage leaves on each of 4 individual plates. Divide slaw equally among plates; garnish with whole green onions, if desired. Season to taste with salt and pepper. Makes 4 servings.

Per serving: *468 calories (24% calories from fat), 13 g total fat, 2 g saturated fat, 0 mg cholesterol, 577 mg sodium, 78 g carbohydrates, 15 g fiber, 16 g protein, 214 mg calcium, 6 mg iron*

Roasted Vegetable Pizzettes

Pizzettes:

1 pound (455 g) mushrooms

2 medium-size onions

1 medium-size eggplant (about 1¼ lbs./565 g)

5 teaspoons (25 ml) olive oil

12 ounces (340 g) pear-shaped (Roma-type) tomatoes (about 4 medium-size tomatoes)

½ cup (85 g) chopped canned roasted red peppers, drained

4 small Italian bread shells (*each* about 5½ inches/13.5 cm in diameter, about 4 oz./115 g); or 4 pita breads (*each* about 5 inches/12.5 cm in diameter)

Dressing:

2 tablespoons (30 ml) balsamic vinegar

1 tablespoon (15 ml) olive oil

1 teaspoon Dijon mustard

Accompaniments:

4 cups (about 3 oz./85 g) lightly packed arugula leaves (tough stems discarded), rinsed and drained

¾ cup (60 g) shaved or shredded Parmesan cheese

Slow-roasted vegetables make a delicious topping for individual pizzas—and you can roast them a day ahead, then spoon them onto purchased bread shells or pita rounds and heat just minutes before mealtime.

Preparation time: 25 minutes   **Cooking time:** About 1 hour and 10 minutes

1 Cut mushrooms into ½-inch (1-cm) slices. Cut onions into wedges about ½ inch (1 cm) thick; cut unpeeled eggplant into about ½-inch (1-cm) cubes.

2 Pour the 5 teaspoons (25 ml) oil into a shallow 10- by 15-inch (25- by 38-cm) baking pan; place in a 450°F (230°C) oven just until oil is hot. Remove pan from oven and add mushrooms, onions, and eggplant; return to oven and bake until vegetables are golden (about 45 minutes), turning vegetables every 15 minutes. Meanwhile, cut tomatoes crosswise into ¼-inch (6-mm) slices.

3 After vegetables have baked for 45 minutes, stir in tomatoes; continue to bake until almost all liquid has evaporated, about 20 more minutes. (At this point, you may let cool, then cover and refrigerate until next day.)

4 Stir red peppers into roasted vegetables. Place bread shells in a single layer on 1 or 2 baking sheets. Spread a fourth of the vegetables evenly over each bread shell (or over each whole pita bread) to within ½ inch (1 cm) of edge.

5 Bake in a 500°F (260°C) oven just until bread and vegetables are heated through (about 5 minutes). Meanwhile, in a small bowl, beat vinegar, the 1 tablespoon (15 ml) oil, and mustard until blended; set aside.

6 To serve, transfer pizzettes to individual plates and top equally with arugula (thinly slice any large arugula pieces) and cheese. Drizzle dressing over all. Makes 4 servings.

Per serving: *572 calories (30% calories from fat), 19 g total fat, 6 g saturated fat, 20 mg cholesterol, 917 mg sodium, 77 g carbohydrates, 9 g fiber, 25 g protein, 390 mg calcium, 6 mg iron*

Potato-Onion Pie

2 slices sourdough sandwich bread, torn into pieces

4 small red thin-skinned potatoes (about 1 lb./455 g *total*), scrubbed

1 large onion

1 tablespoon (15 ml) olive oil

2 teaspoons chopped fresh rosemary or ¾ teaspoon dried rosemary, crumbled

3 large eggs

6 large egg whites

1 cup (240 ml) smooth unsweetened applesauce

⅔ cup (55 g) grated Parmesan cheese

About ¼ teaspoon salt (or to taste)

⅛ teaspoon pepper
Rosemary sprigs

1¼ cups (300 ml) nonfat sour cream

This main-dish pie of rosemary-seasoned onions and red potatoes is good as a lunch or supper entrée; or try it for a weekend brunch.

Preparation time: 20 minutes   **Cooking time:** About 1 hour and 5 minutes

1 In a blender or food processor, whirl bread to make coarse crumbs; set bread crumbs aside.

2 Cut potatoes and onion lengthwise into halves; then thinly slice potato and onion halves crosswise. Heat oil in a wide nonstick frying pan over medium-high heat. Add potatoes, onion, and chopped rosemary. Cook, stirring often, until vegetables are tinged with brown and tender when pierced (20 to 25 minutes); add water, 1 tablespoon (15 ml) at a time, if pan appears dry.

3 Meanwhile, in a medium-size bowl, combine eggs, egg whites, applesauce, cheese, salt, and pepper. Beat until blended; set aside.

4 Spoon potato mixture into a greased deep 9-inch (23-cm) pie pan. Stir crumbs into egg mixture and pour evenly over potato mixture; stir gently so egg mixture settles to pan bottom. Center of filling will be slightly above level of pan.

5 Bake in a 350°F (175°C) oven until top of pie is tinged with brown and a knife inserted in center comes out clean (about 40 minutes). Garnish with rosemary sprigs. Offer sour cream to add to taste. Makes 6 servings.

Per serving: *277 calories (29% calories from fat), 9 g total fat, 3 g saturated fat, 113 mg cholesterol, 441 mg sodium, 31 g carbohydrates, 3 g fiber, 16 g protein, 219 mg calcium, 1 mg iron*

Roasted Zucchini-Mushroom Sandwiches

1 medium-size red onion (about 8 oz./230 g)

1¼ pounds (565 g) zucchini

1¼ pounds (565 g) mushrooms

5 teaspoons (25 ml) olive oil

2 tablespoons (30 ml) balsamic vinegar

12 slices whole wheat sandwich bread

6 thin slices reduced-fat Jarlsberg cheese (about 3 oz./85 g *total*)

¾ cup (180 ml) reduced-fat sour cream

Zucchini, mushrooms, and red onion—oven-browned to develop rich, sweet flavor—are the base of this wholesome sandwich spread.

Preparation time: 30 minutes, plus at least 30 minutes to chill   **Cooking time:** About 30 minutes

1 Cut onion crosswise into ½-inch (1-cm) slices. Cut zucchini lengthwise into ¼-inch (6-mm) slices; cut mushrooms into ½-inch (1-cm) slices. Brush 3 shallow 10- by 15-inch (25- by 38-cm) baking pans with oil, using 1 teaspoon of the oil per pan. Lay onion and zucchini in a single layer in 2 of the pans; spread mushrooms evenly in third pan, overlapping slices as little as possible. Brush onion with all the vinegar; brush all vegetables with remaining 2 teaspoons oil.

2 Bake in a 475°F (245°C) oven for 15 minutes. Turn vegetables over and continue to bake until mushrooms are lightly browned and onion is well browned (about 15 more minutes).

3 Place onion, zucchini, and mushrooms in a food processor or blender; whirl until smoothly puréed. Before using, cover and refrigerate for at least 30 minutes or up to 3 days.

4 To make each sandwich, spread one slice of bread with about ½ cup (120 ml) of the vegetable spread; top with one slice of the cheese, 2 tablespoons (30 ml) of the sour cream, and a second slice of bread. Makes 6 servings.

Per serving: *286 calories (26% calories from fat), 9 g total fat, 2 g saturated fat, 7 mg cholesterol, 380 mg sodium, 39 g carbohydrates, 6 g fiber, 15 g protein, 108 mg calcium, 4 mg iron*

Crustless Spinach Pie *(Pictured on facing page)*

3 slices sourdough sandwich bread, torn into pieces

1 large onion, finely chopped

4 to 6 cloves garlic, minced or pressed

½ cup (120 ml) vegetable broth

About ¾ cup (100 g) crumbled Gorgonzola or other blue-veined cheese

3 tablespoons all-purpose flour

⅛ teaspoon ground white pepper

2 packages (about 10 oz./285 g *each*) frozen chopped spinach, thawed and squeezed dry

1 large egg

6 large egg whites

1½ cups (360 ml) nonfat sour cream

¼ cup (60 ml) smooth unsweetened applesauce

½ teaspoon sugar

⅛ to ¼ teaspoon ground nutmeg

Crisp crumbs top a rich-tasting, Gorgonzola-laced spinach filling in this lean, savory crustless pie.

Preparation time: 15 minutes   **Cooking time:** About 50 minutes

1 In a blender or food processor, whirl bread to make coarse crumbs. Sprinkle ½ cup (23 g) of the crumbs evenly over bottom of a greased 1½- to 2½-quart (1.4- to 2.4-liter) baking dish or deep 9-inch (23-cm) pie pan. Set dish and remaining crumbs aside.

2 In a wide nonstick frying pan, combine onion, garlic, and ¼ cup (60 ml) water. Cook over medium-high heat, stirring often, until onion is soft (about 5 minutes); add water, 1 tablespoon (15 ml) at a time, if pan appears dry. Add broth and cheese; reduce heat to medium and cook, stirring, until cheese is melted. Sprinkle flour and white pepper over cheese mixture and stir until blended. Remove pan from heat and stir in spinach.

3 In a medium-size bowl, whisk egg, egg whites, ½ cup (120 ml) of the sour cream, and applesauce until very well blended. Stir egg mixture into spinach mixture. Spoon into prepared dish; sprinkle with remaining crumbs. Bake in a 375°F (190°C) oven until edge of pie is browned and center feels firm when lightly pressed (about 40 minutes). Let stand for about 5 minutes before serving.

4 Meanwhile, in a small bowl, combine remaining 1 cup (240 ml) sour cream, sugar, and nutmeg. Beat until smoothly blended. To serve, offer sour cream sauce to spoon over pie. Makes 6 servings.

Per serving: *238 calories (29% calories from fat), 8 g total fat, 4 g saturated fat, 52 mg cholesterol, 606 mg sodium, 24 g carbohydrates, 3 g fiber, 18 g protein, 310 mg calcium, 3 mg iron*

Eggplant-Zucchini Lasagne

2 medium-size eggplants (about 2½ lbs./1.15 kg *total*)

4 small zucchini (about 1 lb./455 g *total*)

1 tablespoon (15 ml) olive oil

10 ounces (285 g) firm reduced-fat tofu, rinsed and drained

1½ cups (360 ml) nonfat cottage cheese

1½ cups (about 6 oz./170 g) shredded part-skim mozzarella cheese

1 cup (145 g) cooked brown rice

½ teaspoon fennel seeds, crushed

½ teaspoon crushed red pepper flakes

2½ cups (590 ml) purchased reduced-fat spaghetti sauce

2 tablespoons grated Parmesan cheese

Thin slices of eggplant and zucchini replace the traditional wide noodles in this variation on an old favorite. The filling still features the usual mozzarella and cottage cheeses, but includes tofu and chewy brown rice as well. (Use leftover rice if you have it, or start it cooking before you bake the vegetables.)

Preparation time: 45 minutes   **Cooking time:** About 1¼ hours

1 Cut unpeeled eggplants crosswise into ½-inch (1-cm) slices; cut zucchini lengthwise into ¼-inch (6-mm) slices. Brush 3 shallow 10- by 15-inch (25- by 38-cm) baking pans with oil; arrange vegetable slices in a single layer in pans. Bake in a 400°F (205°C) for 15 minutes; then turn vegetables over and continue to bake until tinged with brown (about 15 more minutes).

2 Meanwhile, slice tofu; place between paper towels and press gently to release excess liquid. Place tofu in a medium-size bowl and mash well. Mix in cottage cheese, mozzarella cheese, rice, fennel seeds, and red pepper flakes.

3 Spread ½ cup (120 ml) of the spaghetti sauce in a 9- by 13-inch (23- by 33-cm) baking pan. Top evenly with half each of the eggplant, zucchini, and tofu mixture; spread with 1 cup (240 ml) more spaghetti sauce. Repeat layers. Sprinkle with Parmesan cheese. Bake in a 400°F (205°C) oven until heated through (about 45 minutes). Let stand for about 10 minutes before serving. Makes 8 servings.

Per serving: *228 calories (26% calories from fat), 7 g total fat, 3 g saturated fat, 17 mg cholesterol, 560 mg sodium, 26 g carbohydrates, 4 g fiber, 17 g protein, 282 mg calcium, 2 mg iron*

Crustless Spinach Pie
(recipe on facing page)

Hot Artichoke Appetizer

Preparation time: *10 minutes*
Cooking time: *50 to 55 minutes*

1   long, slender baguette (about 8 oz./230 g, about 25 inches/63 cm long), cut diagonally into 24 slices
½   cup (40 g) grated Parmesan cheese
1   large package (about 8 oz./230 g) Neufchâtel cheese or regular cream cheese, at room temperature
¾   cup (180 ml) low-fat (2%) cottage cheese
1   cup (240 ml) nonfat sour cream
⅛   teaspoon dried dill weed (or to taste)
2   cans (about 14 oz./400 g *each*) artichoke hearts, drained and chopped

Arrange bread slices in a single layer (overlapping as little as possible) in shallow 10- by 15-inch (25- by 38-cm) baking pans. Bake in a 325°F (165°C) oven until crisp and tinged with brown (15 to 20 minutes). Transfer toast to a rack to cool.

In a large bowl, combine Parmesan cheese, Neufchâtel cheese, cottage cheese, sour cream, and dill weed. Beat with an electric mixer until smooth (or whirl in a food processor or blender until smooth).

Reserve about a fourth of the artichokes. With a spoon, stir remaining artichokes into cheese mixture until evenly distributed.

Transfer cheese-artichoke mixture to a shallow 4- to 5-cup (950-ml to 1.2-liter) baking dish; bake in a 325°F (165°C) oven until lightly browned (about 30 minutes).

Appetizers

✳

Sprinkle with reserved artichokes and return to oven for about 5 minutes. Serve with toast. Makes 12 servings.

Per serving: 212 calories (30% calories from fat), 7 g total fat , 4 g saturated fat, 19 mg cholesterol, 452 mg sodium, 25 g carbohydrates, 1 g fiber, 11 g protein, 143 mg calcium, 2 mg iron

✳

Lentils with Green Herbs

Preparation time: *30 minutes*
Cooking time: *About 1 hour*

1   cup (200 g) lentils
1   large onion, finely chopped
2½ cups (590 ml) vegetable broth
1   can (about 4 oz./115 g) diced green chiles
1   tablespoon mustard seeds
½   teaspoon coriander seeds
½   teaspoon grated lime or lemon peel
¼   teaspoon cumin seeds
½   cup (20 g) *each* fresh mint leaves and cilantro leaves
2   tablespoons (30 ml) lime juice
    Thin lime slices and cilantro sprigs

12 miniature whole wheat or regular pita breads (*each* about 3 inches/8 cm in diameter), cut into halves
½   cup (120 ml) plain nonfat yogurt

Sort through lentils, discarding any debris. Rinse and drain lentils; set aside.

In a 5- to 6-quart (5- to 6-liter) pan, combine onion and ½ cup (120 ml) of the broth. Cook over medium-high heat, stirring often, until liquid evaporates and browned bits stick to pan bottom (about 10 minutes). To deglaze pan, add ⅓ cup (80 ml) water, stirring to loosen browned bits from pan; continue to cook until browned bits form again. Repeat deglazing step about 2 more times or until onion is browned, using ⅓ cup (80 ml) water each time.

To pan, add remaining 2 cups (470 ml) broth, chiles, mustard seeds, coriander seeds, lime peel, cumin seeds, and lentils. Bring to a boil over high heat; then reduce heat, cover, and simmer until lentils are tender to bite (about 35 minutes).

Drain and reserve any cooking liquid. Let lentils cool.

Meanwhile, in a food processor or blender, whirl mint leaves and cilantro leaves until finely chopped (or finely chop with a knife). Add chopped herbs and lime juice to lentils; if you want moister lentils, add a little of the reserved cooking liquid.

Transfer lentils to a bowl and garnish with lime slices and cilantro sprigs. To eat, spoon mixture into pita breads and add yogurt to taste. Makes 12 servings.

Per serving: 157 calories (6% calories from fat), 1 g total fat, 0 g saturated fat, 0 mg cholesterol, 435 mg sodium, 29 g carbohydrates, 3 g fiber, 8 g protein, 64 mg calcium, 2 mg iron

Grilled Vegetable Appetizer

Preparation time: *25 minutes*
Cooking time: *About 1½ hours, including time to heat grill*

2   long, slender baguettes (*each about 8 oz./230 g, about 25 inches/63 cm long), cut diagonally into slices about 1 inch (2.5 cm) thick

4   medium-size slender eggplants, such as Asian or Italian (about 12 oz./340 g *total*)

3   medium-size sweet potatoes or yams (about 1¼ lbs./565 g *total*), scrubbed

1   large onion

3   tablespoons (45 ml) olive oil

2   large red bell peppers (about 1¼ lbs./565 g *total*), seeded

3   large heads garlic (about 12 oz./340 g *total*), unpeeled (leave heads whole)

1½ teaspoons chopped fresh rosemary or ½ teaspoon dried rosemary, crumbled

1½ teaspoons chopped fresh sage or ½ teaspoon dried rubbed sage

Rosemary sprigs and fresh sage leaves

Salt and pepper

Arrange bread slices in a single layer (overlapping as little as possible) in shallow 10- by 15-inch (25- by 38-cm) baking pans. Bake in a 325°F (165°C) oven until crisp and tinged with brown (15 to 20 minutes). Transfer toast to a rack to cool.

While bread is toasting, ignite 70 charcoal briquets in a large barbecue with dampers open. Spread coals out in a solid layer and let burn until medium-low to low; if fire is too hot, vegetables will scorch.

Cut ends from eggplants and sweet potatoes; cut unpeeled onion into quarters. Brush cut surfaces of onion with a little of the oil. Place eggplants, sweet potatoes, onion, bell peppers, and garlic on a greased grill 4 to 6 inches above coals. Cover barbecue. Cook until vegetables are very tender when pressed, watching carefully to prevent scorching; allow about 40 minutes for eggplant and peppers, 50 to 60 minutes for onion and garlic, and 1 hour for sweet potatoes. During the first 30 minutes of grilling, turn vegetables every 5 minutes; after 30 minutes, add 10 more briquets to the fire and turn vegetables every 10 minutes. Remove vegetables from grill as they are cooked.

Remove peel from sweet potatoes, onion, and bell peppers. Cut heads of garlic in half horizontally. Coarsely chop eggplants, peppers, and sweet potatoes. Squeeze half the garlic cloves from skins and finely chop.

On a platter, arrange chopped eggplants, peppers, and sweet potatoes; onion quarters; and whole garlic cloves. Place chopped garlic in center of platter.

Drizzle vegetables with remaining oil; sprinkle with chopped rosemary and sage. Garnish with rosemary sprigs and sage leaves. Place toast in a basket. Serve; or, if made ahead, cover lightly and let stand for up to 2 hours.

To serve, top toast with garlic (either chopped or whole cloves); then spoon other vegetables on top. Season to taste with salt and pepper. Makes 8 servings.

Per serving: 376 calories (17% calories from fat), 7 g total fat, 1 g saturated fat, 0 mg cholesterol, 365 mg sodium, 70 g carbohydrates, 7 g fiber, 10 g protein, 157 mg calcium, 3 mg iron

※

White Bean Pâté with Tomato Relish

Preparation time: *20 minutes*
Cooking time: *15 to 20 minutes*

Baguette Toasts:

1   long, slender baguette (about 8 oz./230 g, about 25 inches/63 cm long), cut diagonally into 24 slices

Tomato Relish:

1   large tomato (about 8 oz./230 g), chopped and drained well

1   to 2 tablespoons chopped parsley

1   tablespoon (15 ml) balsamic vinegar

1   tablespoon drained capers

½   teaspoon sugar

Pepper

White Bean Pâté:

1   can (about 15 oz./425 g) cannellini (white kidney beans), drained and rinsed

1½ teaspoons Oriental sesame oil

¾   teaspoon chopped fresh thyme or ¼ teaspoon dried thyme

¼   teaspoon grated lemon peel

4   teaspoons lemon juice

1   clove garlic, peeled

¼   teaspoon salt (or to taste)

Thyme sprigs

Arrange bread slices in a single layer (overlapping as little as possible) in shallow 10- by 15-inch (25- by 38-cm) baking pans. Bake in a 325°F (165°C) oven until crisp and tinged with brown (15 to 20 minutes). Transfer toast to a rack to cool.

In a small bowl, stir together tomato, parsley, vinegar, capers, and sugar; season to taste with pepper. Set aside; stir occasionally.

In a blender or food processor, combine beans, oil, chopped thyme, lemon peel, lemon juice, garlic, and salt. Whirl until almost smooth. Spoon bean pâté into a small serving bowl or crock and garnish with thyme sprigs.

Offer bean pâté to spread over toast. Spoon tomato relish over pâté, using a slotted spoon. Makes 8 to 12 servings.

Per serving: 86 calories (14% calories from fat), 1 g total fat, 0.2 g saturated fat, 0 mg cholesterol, 224 mg sodium, 15 g carbohydrates, 2 g fiber, 4 g protein, 25 mg calcium, 0.9 mg iron

Corn Pancakes with Black Bean Salsa
(recipe on facing page)

Corn Pancakes with Black Bean Salsa *(Pictured on facing page)*

Black Bean Salsa:

- 1 can (about 15 oz./425 g) black beans, drained and rinsed well
- 1 cup (115 g) peeled, finely chopped jicama
- ¾ cup (100 g) crumbled feta cheese
- 3 tablespoons (45 ml) lime juice
- ⅓ cup (15 g) chopped cilantro
- 2 tablespoons sliced green onion
- 2 teaspoons honey
- ¼ teaspoon crushed red pepper flakes

Corn Pancakes:

- 1 tablespoon butter or margarine
- 1 package (about 10 oz./285 g) frozen corn kernels, thawed and drained
- 1 large egg
- ⅓ cup (50 g) diced red bell pepper
- ⅓ cup (80 ml) nonfat milk
- 3 tablespoons yellow cornmeal
- ⅓ cup (40 g) all-purpose flour
- 1½ teaspoons *each* sugar and baking powder

Garnishes:

- Cilantro sprigs (optional)
- Lime wedges

A zesty black bean salsa, tangy with lime and feta cheese, accompanies savory cornmeal pancakes studded with whole corn kernels.

Preparation time: 20 minutes **Cooking time:** About 6 minutes

1 To prepare salsa, in a large bowl, combine beans, jicama, cheese, lime juice, chopped cilantro, onion, honey, and red pepper flakes. Cover and set aside; stir occasionally.

2 To prepare pancakes, melt butter in a wide nonstick frying pan over low heat. Remove pan from heat. Transfer butter to a large bowl (do not wash frying pan) and add corn, egg, bell pepper, and milk; mix well. In a small bowl, stir together cornmeal, flour, sugar, and baking powder. Add cornmeal mixture to corn mixture and stir just until dry ingredients are evenly moistened.

3 Place frying pan over medium-high heat. When pan is hot, drop batter into pan in 3-tablespoon (45-ml) portions, spacing portions of batter about 3 inches (8 cm) apart. Use a spoon to spread each portion into about a 3-inch (8-cm) circle. Cook pancakes until tops look dry and bottoms are lightly browned (1 to 2 minutes); turn pancakes with a wide spatula and continue to cook until lightly browned on other side (about 1 more minute). As pancakes are cooked, transfer them to a platter and keep warm.

4 Garnish pancakes with cilantro sprigs (if desired) and lime wedges; serve with black bean salsa to add to taste. Makes 4 servings.

Per serving: *336 calories (28% calories from fat), 11 g total fat, 6 g saturated fat, 84 mg cholesterol, 700 mg sodium, 49 g carbohydrates, 6 g fiber, 14 g protein, 294 mg calcium, 3 mg iron*

Zucchini-Carrot Pizza

- 1 cup (100 g) fine dry bread crumbs
- 1 teaspoon olive oil
- 2 cloves garlic, minced or pressed
- 1 large egg
- 2 large egg whites
- 2 tablespoons all-purpose flour
- ¼ teaspoon pepper
- 1 teaspoon dried basil
- 1 cup (100 g) shredded carrots
- 1 cup (100 g) shredded zucchini
- 1 teaspoon yellow cornmeal
- ¾ cup (85 g) shredded reduced-fat jack cheese
- 1 cup (70 g) very thinly sliced mushrooms

This pizza's crisp crust isn't made from the usual yeast dough; instead, it's based on an herb-seasoned combination of shredded zucchini, carrots, and bread crumbs. Embellish the baked crust with creamy jack cheese and fresh mushrooms to make an entrée both adults and children will enjoy.

Preparation time: 15 minutes **Cooking time:** About 40 minutes

1 In a wide nonstick frying pan, combine bread crumbs, oil, and garlic. Stir over medium-high heat until crumbs are crisp (about 6 minutes). Remove from pan and set aside.

2 In a large bowl, combine egg, egg whites, flour, pepper, basil, carrots, and zucchini. Mix until evenly blended. Add crumbs and mix well. Sprinkle a 12-inch (30-cm) nonstick or regular pizza pan with cornmeal. Spread vegetable mixture evenly in pan and bake in a 400°F (205°C) oven until browned (about 20 minutes).

3 Sprinkle crust with cheese and mushrooms and continue to bake until cheese is melted (about 10 minutes). Makes 4 servings.

Per serving: *261 calories (27% calories from fat), 8 g total fat, 4 g saturated fat, 68 mg cholesterol, 459 mg sodium, 32 g carbohydrates, 3 g fiber, 16 g protein, 287 mg calcium, 3 mg iron*

Potato Curry

Spice Mixture:

2   tablespoons ground coriander

1   tablespoon ground cumin

½   teaspoon ground turmeric

¼   to ½ teaspoon ground red pepper (cayenne), or to taste

¼   teaspoon ground cinnamon

Potato Curry:

    About 5 cups (1.2 liters) vegetable broth

2   large onions, chopped

4   cloves garlic, minced or pressed

2   tablespoons finely chopped fresh ginger

¼   teaspoon coconut extract

3   large russet potatoes (about 1½ lbs./680 g *total*)

2   very large sweet potatoes or yams (about 1½ lbs./680 g *total*)

1   pound (455 g) broccoli flowerets (about 7 cups), cut into bite-size pieces

1   cup (240 ml) nonfat milk

1   package (about 10 oz./285 g) frozen tiny peas, thawed and drained

Accompaniments:

¼   cup (30 g) salted roasted cashew pieces

½   cup (20 g) cilantro leaves

2   cups (470 ml) plain nonfat yogurt

Broccoli, green peas, and both russet and sweet potatoes simmer in an aromatic curry sauce to make this hearty stew. Serve it over hot brown rice; complete the meal with cooling fresh fruit.

Preparation time: 30 minutes   **Cooking time:** About 1½ hours

1 To prepare spice mixture, combine coriander, cumin, turmeric, red pepper, and cinnamon in a 5- to 6-quart (5- to 6-liter) pan. Cook over medium-low heat, stirring, until spices are fragrant (about 5 minutes; do not scorch). Remove from pan and set aside.

2 In same pan, combine ½ cup (120 ml) of the broth, onions, garlic, and ginger. Cook over medium-high heat, stirring often, until liquid evaporates and browned bits stick to pan bottom (about 10 minutes). To deglaze pan, add ⅓ cup (80 ml) more broth, stirring to loosen browned bits from pan; continue to cook until browned bits form again. Repeat deglazing step about 2 more times or until vegetables are browned, using ⅓ cup (80 ml) more broth each time. Add spice mixture and repeat deglazing step one more time, using ⅓ cup (80 ml) more broth. Remove from heat.

3 Add coconut extract and 3 cups (710 ml) more broth to pan. Peel russet and sweet potatoes, cut into 1½- to 2-inch (4- to 5-cm) chunks, and add to broth mixture. Bring to a boil over high heat; then reduce heat, cover, and simmer until potatoes are tender when pierced (about 35 minutes). Add broccoli, cover, and continue to cook for 10 more minutes. Add milk and peas; simmer, uncovered, stirring occasionally, just until stew is hot (do not boil).

4 Pour stew into a serving bowl. Sprinkle with cashews and cilantro. Offer yogurt to add to taste. Makes 6 servings.

Per serving: 360 calories (11% calories from fat), 4 g total fat, 1 g saturated fat, 2 mg cholesterol, 1,015 mg sodium, 68 g carbohydrates, 9 g fiber, 16 g protein, 294 mg calcium, 4 mg iron

Sweet Potato-Fennel Gratin

3 heads fennel (*each* 3 to 4 inches/8 to 10 cm in diameter; about 2 lbs./905 g *total*)

2 large onions, chopped

1 teaspoon fennel seeds, crushed
About 4 cups (950 ml) vegetable broth

¼ cup (30 g) all-purpose flour

¼ teaspoon ground nutmeg

½ cup (120 ml) half-and-half

4 very large sweet potatoes or yams (about 3 lbs./1.35 kg *total*)

3 cups (about 12 oz./340 g) shredded reduced-fat Jarlsberg cheese

This unusual gratin is made with layers of sweet potato slices, buttery-rich Jarlsberg cheese, and braised fennel. A seasoning of fennel seeds brings out the fresh vegetable's mild licorice flavor.

Preparation time: 45 minutes   **Cooking time:** About 2¼ hours

1 Trim stems from fennel; reserve some of the feathery leaves for garnish. Discard stems. Trim and discard discolored parts of fennel. Finely chop fennel.

2 In a 5- to 6-quart (5- to 6-liter) pan, combine chopped fennel, onions, fennel seeds, and ½ cup (120 ml) of the broth. Cook over medium-high heat, stirring often, until liquid evaporates and browned bits stick to pan bottom (about 10 minutes). To deglaze pan, add ⅓ cup (80 ml) more broth, stirring to loosen browned bits from pan; continue to cook until browned bits form again. Repeat deglazing step about 3 more times or until vegetables are browned, using ⅓ cup (80 ml) more broth each time. Add flour and nutmeg to vegetables; mix well. Add half-and-half and 2 cups (470 ml) more broth; stir over medium heat until mixture comes to a boil (about 5 minutes). Remove from heat.

3 Peel sweet potatoes and thinly slice crosswise. Arrange a fourth of the fennel mixture in a 9- by 13-inch (23- by 33-cm) baking pan. Cover with a fourth of the sweet potatoes and ¾ cup (85 g) of the cheese. Repeat layers 2 more times. Add remaining fennel mixture in an even layer; top evenly with remaining sweet potatoes. Reserve remaining ¾ cup (85 g) cheese.

4 Cover tightly and bake in a 350°F (175°C) oven for 45 minutes; then uncover and sprinkle with remaining ¾ cup (85 g) cheese. Continue to bake, uncovered, until potatoes are tender when pierced and top of casserole is golden brown (about 1 more hour). Garnish with reserved fennel leaves. Makes 8 to 10 servings.

Per serving: *294 calories (25% calories from fat), 8 g total fat, 4 g saturated fat, 25 mg cholesterol, 679 mg sodium, 39 g carbohydrates, 5 g fiber, 15 g protein, 91 mg calcium, 2 mg iron*

Eggplant & Cheese Casserole

3 small eggplants (about 3 lbs./1.35 kg *total*)

1 large onion, chopped

1 large green bell pepper (about 8 oz./230 g), seeded and chopped

¾ cup (75 g) fine dry bread crumbs

1 can (about 2¼ oz./63 g) sliced ripe olives, drained

1 tablespoon chopped fresh oregano or 1 teaspoon dried oregano

1 large can (about 15 oz./425 g) tomato sauce

1 cup (about 8 oz./230 g) nonfat ricotta cheese

1½ cups (about 6 oz./170 g) shredded reduced-fat sharp Cheddar cheese

To make this rich, layered casserole, start by baking a savory mixture of diced eggplant and olives in tomato sauce; then top with spoonfuls of ricotta cheese and a generous helping of sharp Cheddar. Bake for another 10 minutes or so and serve hot, with a salad and crunchy breadsticks.

Preparation time: 25 minutes   **Cooking time:** About 1 hour and 40 minutes

1 Cut unpeeled eggplants into ¾-inch (2-cm) cubes and place in a deep 4-quart (3.8-liter) casserole. Add onion, bell pepper, bread crumbs, olives, oregano, and tomato sauce; stir well. Cover tightly and bake in a 400°F (205°C) oven for 45 minutes. Stir vegetables thoroughly and cover tightly again. Continue to bake until vegetables are very soft when pressed (about 45 more minutes); check occasionally and add water, 1 tablespoon (15 ml) at a time, if casserole appears dry.

2 Spoon ricotta cheese in dollops over hot vegetable mixture; sprinkle with Cheddar cheese. Continue to bake, uncovered, until Cheddar cheese is melted (about 10 more minutes). Makes 8 servings.

Per serving: *212 calories (23% calories from fat), 5 g total fat, 3 g saturated fat, 15 mg cholesterol, 687 mg sodium, 27 g carbohydrates, 5 g fiber, 15 g protein, 447 mg calcium, 2 mg iron*

Broccoli-Cornmeal Kuchen *(Pictured on facing page)*

Kuchen:

3½ cups (about 8 oz./230 g) broccoli flowerets

½ cup (69 g) yellow cornmeal

½ cup (60 g) all-purpose flour

1½ teaspoons baking powder

1 cup (240 ml) nonfat cottage cheese

1 large egg

3 large egg whites

½ cup (120 ml) low-fat buttermilk

2 tablespoons butter or margarine, melted

4 teaspoons sugar

Yogurt Sauce:

1 cup (240 ml) plain nonfat yogurt

¼ cup (60 ml) white wine vinegar

2 tablespoons dried dill weed (or to taste)

1 teaspoon honey (or to taste)

¼ teaspoon ground cumin

Kuchen is traditionally a sweet, fruit- or cheese-filled yeast coffeecake served for dessert or at breakfast, but this savory version is meant to be enjoyed as a lunch or supper main dish. It's nutritious, easy to prepare—and pretty, too.

Preparation time: 20 minutes   **Cooking time:** About 40 minutes

1. In a 4- to 5-quart (3.8- to 5-liter) pan, bring 8 cups (1.9 liters) water to a boil over medium-high heat. Add broccoli and cook just until barely tender-crisp to bite (about 4 minutes). Drain, immerse in ice water until cool, and drain well again.

2. In a large bowl, stir together cornmeal, flour, and baking powder. In a small bowl, beat cottage cheese, egg, egg whites, buttermilk, butter, and sugar until well blended. Add cheese mixture to cornmeal mixture and stir just until dry ingredients are evenly moistened.

3. Pour batter into a greased 8-inch-round (20-cm-round) baking pan or quiche dish. Gently press broccoli decoratively into batter. Bake in a 350°F (175°C) oven until center of kuchen feels firm when lightly pressed (about 30 minutes).

4. Meanwhile, in a small bowl, stir together yogurt, vinegar, dill weed, honey, and cumin just until blended. Set aside.

5. Let kuchen cool slightly; then cut into wedges. Offer yogurt sauce to spoon over individual portions. Makes 4 servings.

Per serving: *303 calories (27% calories from fat), 9 g total fat, 4 g saturated fat, 72 mg cholesterol, 390 mg sodium, 42 g carbohydrates, 3 g fiber, 14 g protein, 282 mg calcium, 3 mg iron*

Broccoli Burgers

Red Onion Relish:

2 medium-size red onions (about 1 lb./455 g *total*), chopped

2 tablespoons firmly packed brown sugar

1 teaspoon olive oil

⅓ cup (80 ml) *each* balsamic vinegar and dry white wine

2 teaspoons prepared horseradish

Broccoli Burgers:

2 large eggs, lightly beaten

1¾ cups (125 g) chopped broccoli

½ cup (65 g) chopped toasted almonds

¾ cup (130 g) chopped red onion

½ cup (50 g) seasoned fine dry bread crumbs

Salt and pepper

¼ cup (60 ml) nonfat mayonnaise

4 hamburger buns, toasted

4 to 8 lettuce leaves, rinsed and crisped

Enjoy a low-fat, no-meat version of a favorite fast food with these veggie burgers, chock-full of broccoli, red onion, and toasted almonds. Serve them with nonfat mayonnaise and a tangy homemade relish.

Preparation time: 15 minutes   **Cooking time:** About 45 minutes

1. In a wide nonstick frying pan, combine the 2 chopped onions, sugar, oil, and ½ cup (120 ml) water. Cook over medium-high heat, stirring often, until onions are soft (about 8 minutes); add more water, 1 tablespoon (15 ml) at a time, if pan appears dry. Stir in vinegar, wine, and horseradish. Cook, stirring often, until liquid has evaporated (about 10 minutes). Transfer relish to a small bowl and set aside; stir occasionally.

2. In a large bowl, combine eggs, broccoli, almonds, the ¾ cup onion, bread crumbs, and ¼ cup (60 ml) water. Season to taste with salt and pepper. On an oiled 12- by 15-inch (30- by 38-cm) baking sheet, shape mixture into 4 equal patties, each about ¾ inch (2 cm) thick. Bake patties in a 375°F (190°C) oven, turning halfway through baking, until golden on both sides (about 25 minutes).

3. To serve, spread mayonnaise on bun bottoms; top with patties, onion relish, and lettuce, then with bun tops. Makes 4 servings.

Per serving: *440 calories (30% calories from fat), 15 g total fat, 2 g saturated fat, 106 mg cholesterol, 808 mg sodium, 61 g carbohydrates, 7 g fiber, 16 g protein, 207 mg calcium, 4 mg iron*

Broccoli-Cornmeal Kuchen
(recipe on facing page)

Greek-style Chicken & Potato Salad

Preparation time: *15 minutes, plus at least 15 minutes to chill*

Cooking time: *About 30 minutes*

2   pounds (905 g) small red thin-skinned potatoes (*each about 1½ inches / 3.5 cm in diameter*), scrubbed

1   boneless, skinless chicken breast half (about 6 oz. / 170 g)

1   jar (about 6 oz. / 170 g) marinated artichoke hearts

1   large jar (about 4 oz. / 115 g) sliced pimentos

1   can (about 2¼ oz. / 63 g) sliced ripe olives, drained

½   cup (50 g) thinly sliced green onions

¼   cup (60 ml) lemon juice

4   large romaine lettuce leaves, rinsed and crisped

½   cup (65 g) crumbled feta cheese

Pepper

In a 4- to 5-quart (3.8- to 5-liter) pan, bring 8 cups (1.9 liters) water to a boil over medium-high heat. Add potatoes; reduce heat, cover, and simmer until potatoes are tender when pierced (about 25 minutes). Drain potatoes and let stand until cool enough to handle; then cut into quarters.

While potatoes are cooking, rinse chicken and pat dry. Then, in a 3- to 4-quart (2.8- to 3.8-liter) pan with a tight-fitting lid, bring 8 cups (1.9 liters) water to a rolling boil over high heat. Remove pan from heat and immediately add chicken. Cover pan tightly and let stand until meat in thickest part is no longer pink; cut to test (15 to 20 minutes; do not uncover until ready to test). If chicken is not done, return it to hot water, cover, and steep for 2 to 3 more minutes.

Almost All Vegetables

✳

Lift chicken from pan and let stand just until cool enough to handle; then cut into bite-size pieces. Place in a large bowl and add potatoes, artichokes and their marinade, pimentos, olives, onions, and lemon juice. Mix gently but thoroughly. Cover and refrigerate for at least 15 minutes or up to 4 hours before serving.

To serve, place one lettuce leaf on each of 4 individual plates; divide chicken mixture equally among plates. Sprinkle salads with cheese; season to taste with pepper. Makes 4 servings.

Per serving: 361 calories (26% calories from fat), 11 g total fat, 4 g saturated fat, 44 mg cholesterol, 651 mg sodium, 50 g carbohydrates, 5 g fiber, 19 g protein, 150 mg calcium, 4 mg iron

✳

Shrimp & Avocado Tostadas with Papaya Salsa

Preparation time: *35 minutes*
Cooking time: *About 8 minutes*

Crisp Taco Shells:

4   corn tortillas (*each about 6 inches / 15 cm in diameter*)

Salt (optional)

Papaya Salsa:

1   medium-size firm-ripe papaya (about 1 lb. / 455 g), peeled, seeded, and diced

1   small cucumber (about 8 oz. / 230 g), peeled, seeded, and diced

1   tablespoon chopped fresh mint (or to taste)

2   tablespoons (30 ml) lime juice

1   tablespoon (15 ml) honey

Avocado & Shrimp Topping:

1   teaspoon grated lemon peel

2   tablespoons (30 ml) lemon juice

1   medium-size soft-ripe avocado

1   cup (240 ml) low-fat (2%) cottage cheese

2   or 3 cloves garlic, peeled

⅛   teaspoon salt

2   tablespoons finely chopped cilantro

1   small fresh jalapeño or serrano chile, seeded and finely chopped

1   tablespoon thinly sliced green onion

1   large tomato (about 8 oz. / 230 g), finely chopped and drained well

4   cups (about 4 oz. / 115 g) shredded lettuce

6   ounces (170 g) small cooked shrimp

Dip tortillas, one at a time, in hot water; drain briefly. Season to taste with salt, if desired. Arrange tortillas, not overlapping, in a single layer on a large baking sheet. Bake in a 500°F (260°C) oven for 6 minutes. With a metal spatula, turn tortillas over; continue to bake until crisp and tinged with brown (about 2 more minutes). If made ahead, let cool completely; then store airtight at room temperature until next day.

In a medium-size bowl, stir together papaya, cucumber, mint, lime juice, and honey; set aside. If made ahead, cover and refrigerate for up to 4 hours.

Place lemon peel and lemon juice in a blender or food processor. Halve and pit avocado; scoop flesh from peel into blender. Add cottage cheese, garlic, and the ⅛ teaspoon salt. Whirl until smoothly puréed. With a spoon, gently stir in cilantro, chile, onion, and half the tomato.

To serve, place one taco shell on each of 4 individual plates. Evenly top taco shells with avocado mixture; then top shells equally with lettuce, shrimp, and remaining tomato. Offer papaya salsa to add to taste. Makes 4 servings.

Per serving: 308 calories (29% calories from fat), 10 g total fat, 2 g saturated fat, 87 mg cholesterol, 387 mg sodium, 37 g carbohydrates, 4 g fiber, 21 g protein, 179 mg calcium, 4 mg iron

Autumn Harvest Gratin

Preparation time: *15 minutes*
Cooking time: *About 1 hour and 50 minutes*

3 large sweet potatoes or yams (about 1½ lbs./680 g *total*), peeled

1 cup (240 ml) apple juice
About ½ teaspoon cider vinegar (or to taste)

2 large tart apples such as Newtown Pippin or Granny Smith (about 1 lb./455 g *total*)

1 tablespoon firmly packed brown sugar

4 ounces (115 g) prosciutto, cut into thin strips about 1 inch (2.5 cm) long

1 tablespoon finely chopped fresh oregano or parsley

1 cup (240 ml) plain nonfat yogurt

In a 4- to 5-quart (3.8- to 5-liter) pan, bring 8 cups (1.9 liters) water to a boil over medium-high heat. Add potatoes; then reduce heat, cover, and simmer for 20 minutes. Meanwhile, in a small pan, bring apple juice to a boil over high heat. Boil until reduced to ⅔ cup/160 ml (about 8 minutes). Stir in vinegar and set aside.

Drain potatoes well and let stand until cool enough to handle; then peel and cut into slices about ⅝ inch (1.5 cm) thick. Set aside. Peel and core apples, then cut into slices about ½ inch (1 cm) thick.

Decoratively arrange potato and apple slices in a greased oval 2-quart (1.9-liter) casserole, about 8 by 12 inches (20 by 30 cm). Pour apple juice mixture over potato mixture and sprinkle with sugar. Cover tightly and bake in a 375°F (190°C) oven for 45 minutes.

Uncover casserole and spoon pan juices over potatoes and apples. Return to oven and bake, uncovered, basting occasionally with pan juices, until vegetables are very soft when pierced and almost all liquid has evaporated (30 to 40 more minutes). Ten minutes before casserole is done, sprinkle prosciutto over top; when vegetables are done, prosciutto should be crisp and tinged with brown. Sprinkle with oregano; offer yogurt to add to taste. Makes 4 servings.

Per serving: 328 calories (16% calories from fat), 6 g total fat, 2 g saturated fat, 24 mg cholesterol, 586 mg sodium, 58 g carbohydrates, 6 g fiber, 14 g protein, 154 mg calcium, 2 mg iron

Corn Stew with Cornbread Topping

Preparation time: *15 minutes*
Cooking time: *About 35 minutes*

Corn Stew:

6 ounces (170 g) turkey or pork Italian sausage (casings removed), coarsely chopped

1 can (about 15 oz./425 g) cream-style corn

1 package (about 10 oz./285 g) frozen corn kernels, thawed and drained

1 can (about 4 oz./115 g) diced green chiles

½ teaspoon cumin seeds

Cornbread Topping:

½ cup (69 g) yellow cornmeal

½ cup (60 g) all-purpose flour

2 teaspoons baking powder

⅛ teaspoon salt

1 large egg

½ cup (120 ml) low-fat buttermilk

4 teaspoons (20 ml) honey

1 tablespoon butter or margarine, melted

Garnish:

½ cup (20 g) cilantro leaves

In a small nonstick frying pan, cook sausage over medium-high heat, stirring often, until no longer pink (5 to 7 minutes). Discard any drippings. Transfer sausage to an oval 2-quart (1.9-liter) casserole, about 8 by 12 inches (20 by 30 cm). Add cream-style corn, corn kernels, chiles, and cumin seeds. Mix gently but thoroughly; set aside.

In a medium-size bowl, stir together cornmeal, flour, baking powder, and salt. In a small bowl, beat egg, buttermilk, honey, and butter until blended. Add egg mixture to cornmeal mixture and stir just until dry ingredients are evenly moistened. Drop batter by spoonfuls over corn mixture, spacing evenly; then gently smooth top so spoonfuls of batter just barely touch each other.

Bake in a 375°F (190°C) oven until topping is tinged with brown and feels firm when lightly pressed (25 to 30 minutes). Let stand for about 5 minutes before serving. Garnish with cilantro. Makes 4 servings.

Per serving: 420 calories (22% calories from fat), 11 g total fat, 4 g saturated fat, 95 mg cholesterol, 1,132 mg sodium, 69 g carbohydrates, 4 g fiber, 18 g protein, 163 mg calcium, 3 mg iron

Southwestern Fettuccine
(recipe on page 24)

PASTA

Pasta dishes are high on any list of lean, high-carbohydrate entrées, so it's no surprise to find that they're ideal for low-fat vegetarian meals. The choices in the following pages range from long-time favorites, such as homey baked Macaroni & Cheese, to more unusual creations. For a tempting variation on a classic sauce, try Bow Ties with Broccoli Pesto; to give familiar ravioli a new look, pair the pasta with tangy Gorgonzola. Or choose a Mediterranean-style casserole of orzo and vegetables, a golden, savory spaghetti pie, or an Asian-inspired combination of tofu and chewy penne in spicy peanut sauce.

Southwestern Fettuccine *(Pictured on page 22)*

12	ounces (340 g) dried fettuccine
1	can (about 15 oz./425 g) cream-style corn
⅔	cup (160 ml) nonfat milk
1	teaspoon salad oil
½	teaspoon cumin seeds
1	small onion, chopped
1	large red or yellow bell pepper (about 8 oz./230 g), seeded and cut into thin strips
1	package (about 10 oz./285 g) frozen corn kernels, thawed and drained
1	cup (about 4 oz./115 g) shredded jalapeño jack cheese
¼	cup (10 g) cilantro leaves
1½	to 2 cups (210 to 285 g) yellow or red cherry tomatoes, cut into halves
	Cilantro sprigs
	Lime wedges
	Salt

This satisfying Tex-Mex pasta sauce is based on bell pepper, corn kernels, and nippy jalapeño jack cheese. To thicken it, we've used rich-tasting cream-style corn, puréed in the blender until smooth.

Preparation time: 15 minutes   **Cooking time:** About 20 minutes

1 In a 5- to 6-quart (5- to 6-liter) pan, bring about 3 quarts (2.8 liters) water to boil over medium-high heat; stir in pasta and cook until just tender to bite, 8 to 10 minutes. (Or cook pasta according to package directions.) Drain pasta well and return to pan; keep warm. While pasta is cooking, whirl cream-style corn and milk in a blender or food processor until smoothly puréed; set aside.

2 Heat oil in a wide nonstick frying pan over medium-high heat. Add cumin seeds, onion, and bell pepper. Cook, stirring often, until onion is soft (about 5 minutes); add water, 1 tablespoon (15 ml) at a time, if pan appears dry. Stir in cream-style corn mixture, corn kernels, and cheese. Reduce heat to medium and cook, stirring, just until cheese is melted.

3 Pour corn-cheese sauce over pasta. Add cilantro leaves; mix gently but thoroughly. Divide pasta among 4 shallow individual bowls; sprinkle with tomatoes. Garnish with cilantro sprigs. Season to taste with lime and salt. Makes 4 servings.

Per serving: *627 calories (21% calories from fat), 15 g total fat, 6 g saturated fat, 112 mg cholesterol, 540 mg sodium, 104 g carbohydrates, 7 g fiber, 25 g protein, 298 mg calcium, 5 mg iron*

Macaroni & Cheese

5	ounces (140 g) soft tofu, rinsed and drained
¾	cup (180 ml) reduced-fat sour cream
½	cup (120 ml) nonfat milk
¼	cup (60 ml) smooth unsweetened applesauce
2	teaspoons chopped fresh thyme or ½ teaspoon dried thyme
1	teaspoon Dijon mustard
⅛	teaspoon ground nutmeg
1	teaspoon olive oil
1	large onion, chopped
3	tablespoons (45 ml) dry white wine
2	cups (about 8 oz./230 g) shredded reduced-fat sharp Cheddar cheese
1	large egg, lightly beaten
2	cups (about 6 oz./170 g) dried elbow macaroni
¼	cup (24 g) toasted wheat germ
1	to 2 tablespoons finely chopped fresh oregano or parsley
	Salt and ground white pepper

Topped with wheat germ and herbs, this lightened-up family favorite features a smooth sauce of Cheddar cheese, tofu, sour cream, and milk.

Preparation time: 20 minutes   **Cooking time:** About 1 hour

1 In a blender or food processor, combine tofu, sour cream, milk, applesauce, thyme, mustard, and nutmeg. Whirl until smoothly puréed; set aside.

2 Heat oil in a 4- to 5-quart (3.8- to 5-liter) pan over medium-high heat. Add onion and cook, stirring often, until soft (about 5 minutes). Add wine; cook, stirring, until almost all liquid has evaporated (about 3 minutes). Remove pan from heat and stir in tofu mixture and cheese; then add egg and stir to mix well.

3 In another 4- to 5-quart (3.8- to 5-liter) pan, bring about 8 cups (1.9 liters) water to a boil over medium-high heat; stir in pasta and cook until just tender to bite, 8 to 10 minutes. (Or cook pasta according to package directions.) Drain pasta well, add to cheese mixture, and mix gently but thoroughly.

4 Spoon pasta mixture into a shallow oval 2- to 2½-quart (1.9- to 2.4-liter) casserole. Cover tightly and bake in a 350°F (175°C) oven for 20 minutes. Uncover and continue to bake until edges are lightly browned and mixture is bubbly (about 25 more minutes). Let stand for about 5 minutes.

5 In a small bowl, mix wheat germ and oregano; sprinkle over pasta. Season to taste with salt and white pepper. Makes 4 servings.

Per serving: *463 calories (28% calories from fat), 14 g total fat, 8 g saturated fat, 94 mg cholesterol, 540 mg sodium, 48 g carbohydrates, 3 g fiber, 33 g protein, 650 mg calcium, 3 mg iron*

Couscous with Ratatouille & Feta Cheese

Ratatouille:

1   small onion, cut into thin slivers

1   small red bell pepper (about 4 oz./115 g), seeded and thinly sliced

1   small eggplant (about 1 lb./455 g), peeled and cut into ½-inch (1-cm) cubes

1   tablespoon chopped fresh basil or ¾ teaspoon dried basil (or to taste)

1½   teaspoons chopped fresh thyme or ½ teaspoon dried thyme (or to taste)

     About ¼ teaspoon *each* salt and pepper (or to taste)

1   small zucchini (about 4 oz./115 g), cut into ¼-inch (6-mm) slices

1   can (about 15 oz./425 g) garbanzo beans, drained and rinsed

1   large tomato (about 8 oz./ 230 g), coarsely chopped

Couscous:

2¼   cups (530 ml) low-fat (1%) milk

1   package (about 10 oz./285 g) couscous

1   cup (about 4½ oz./130 g) crumbled feta cheese

Garnish:

     Basil or thyme sprigs

Flavored with basil and thyme, this garden-fresh specialty features popular ratatouille—a Provençal vegetable stew of eggplant, zucchini, and bell peppers—served with couscous and tangy feta cheese.

Preparation time: 20 minutes   **Cooking time:** About 15 minutes

1 In a wide nonstick frying pan, combine onion, bell pepper, eggplant, chopped basil, chopped thyme, salt, pepper, and ½ cup (120 ml) water. Cover and cook over medium-high heat until vegetables are almost tender when pierced (about 5 minutes). Uncover and add zucchini. Cook, stirring gently, until almost all liquid has evaporated. Add beans and tomato; stir gently just until heated through (about 3 minutes).

2 Meanwhile, in a 2½- to 3-quart (2.4- to 2.8-liter) pan, bring milk just to a boil over medium-high heat. Stir in couscous and ¾ cup (100 g) of the cheese; cover, remove from heat, and let stand until liquid has been absorbed (about 5 minutes).

3 Divide couscous equally among 4 shallow individual bowls. Top with vegetable mixture and sprinkle with remaining ¼ cup (33 g) cheese. Garnish with basil sprigs. Makes 4 servings.

Per serving: *537 calories (19% calories from fat), 11 g total fat, 6 g saturated fat, 36 mg cholesterol, 714 mg sodium, 85 g carbohydrates, 8 g fiber, 24 g protein, 430 mg calcium, 4 mg iron*

Oven-baked Mediterranean Orzo *(Pictured on facing page)*

1 large can (about 28 oz./795 g) tomatoes

About 2 cups (470 ml) vegetable broth

1 teaspoon olive oil

1 large onion, cut into very thin slivers

1 can (about 15 oz./425 g) *each* black beans and cannellini (white kidney beans), drained and rinsed well

1 package (about 9 oz./255 g) frozen artichoke hearts, thawed and drained

½ cup (65 g) dried apricots, cut into halves

⅓ cup (50 g) raisins

About 1 tablespoon drained capers (or to taste)

4 teaspoons chopped fresh basil or 1½ teaspoons dried basil

½ teaspoon fennel seeds, crushed

1½ cups (about 10 oz./285 g) dried orzo or other rice-shaped pasta

½ cup (65 g) crumbled feta cheese

Pepper

This combination of tiny pasta, artichokes, and two kinds of beans is an easy one-dish entrée. Raisins and dried apricots add sweet, sunny flavor.

Preparation time: 20 minutes   **Cooking time:** About 50 minutes

1 Break up tomatoes with a spoon and drain liquid into a 4-cup (950-ml) measure; set tomatoes aside. Add enough of the broth to tomato liquid to make 3 cups (710 ml); set aside.

2 Place oil and onion in an oval 3- to 3½-quart (2.8- to 3.3-liter) casserole, about 9 by 13 inches (23 by 33 cm) and at least 2½ inches (6 cm) deep. Bake in a 450°F (230°C) oven until onion is soft and tinged with brown (about 10 minutes). During baking, stir occasionally to loosen browned bits from casserole bottom; add water, 1 tablespoon (15 ml) at a time, if casserole appears dry.

3 Remove casserole from oven and carefully add tomatoes, broth mixture, black beans, cannellini, artichokes, apricots, raisins, capers, basil, and fennel seeds. Stir to loosen any browned bits from casserole. Return to oven and continue to bake until mixture comes to a rolling boil (about 20 minutes).

4 Remove casserole from oven and carefully stir in pasta, scraping casserole bottom to loosen any browned bits. Cover tightly, return to oven, and bake for 10 more minutes; then stir pasta mixture well, scraping casserole bottom. Cover tightly again and continue to bake until pasta is just tender to bite and almost all liquid has been absorbed (about 10 more minutes). Sprinkle with cheese, cover, and let stand for about 5 minutes before serving. Season to taste with pepper. Makes 6 to 8 servings.

Per serving: *358 calories (12% calories from fat), 5 g total fat, 2 g saturated fat, 9 mg cholesterol, 807 mg sodium, 66 g carbohydrates, 9 g fiber, 15 g protein, 140 mg calcium, 5 mg iron*

Goat Cheese–Spinach Pasta

12 ounces (340 g) dried spinach fettuccine

3 quarts (about 12 oz./340 g) lightly packed rinsed, drained fresh spinach leaves, cut or torn into 2-inch (5-cm) pieces

⅔ cup (160 ml) vegetable broth

8 ounces (230 g) unsweetened soft fresh goat cheese (plain or flavored), broken into chunks, if possible (some types may be too soft to break)

2 cups (285 g) ripe cherry tomatoes (at room temperature), cut into ⅓-inch (1-cm) slices

Salt and pepper

Made from pure white goat's milk, goat cheese (often marketed under its French name, chèvre) is distinguished by its unique, delightfully tart flavor. In this recipe, it's melted into a smooth sauce to serve over pasta and spinach.

Preparation time: 15 to 20 minutes   **Cooking time:** About 15 minutes

1 In a 5- to 6-quart (5- to 6-liter) pan, bring about 3 quarts water to a boil over medium-high heat; stir in pasta and cook until just tender to bite, 8 to 10 minutes. (Or cook pasta according to package directions.) Stir spinach into boiling water with pasta; continue to boil until spinach is wilted (30 to 45 more seconds). Drain pasta-spinach mixture well and return to pan.

2 While pasta is cooking, bring broth to a boil in a 1- to 2-quart (950-ml to 1.9-liter) pan over medium-high heat. Add cheese and stir until melted; remove from heat.

3 Spoon cheese mixture over pasta and spinach; mix gently but thoroughly. Spoon onto a platter; scatter tomatoes over top. Season to taste with salt and pepper. Makes 4 servings.

Per serving: *537 calories (28% calories from fat), 17 g total fat, 9 g saturated fat, 107 mg cholesterol, 617 mg sodium, 70 g carbohydrates, 12 g fiber, 30 g protein, 351 mg calcium, 11 mg iron*

Oven-baked Mediterranean Orzo
(recipe on facing page)

Squash & Sweet Potato Soup

Preparation time: *20 minutes*
Cooking time: *About 35 minutes*

Soup:

About 1¾ pounds (795 g) butternut or other gold-fleshed squash

3 very large sweet potatoes or yams (about 1¾ lbs./795 g *total*)

7 cups (1.6 liters) vegetable broth

¼ cup (60 ml) balsamic vinegar

2 tablespoons firmly packed brown sugar

1 tablespoon finely chopped fresh ginger

About ⅛ teaspoon crushed red pepper flakes (or to taste)

Croutons:

1 tablespoon (15 ml) olive oil

1 clove garlic, minced or pressed

3 slices French or sourdough sandwich bread

Salt and pepper

Cut peel from squash; discard seeds. Peel potatoes. Cut squash and potatoes into 1-inch (2.5-cm) pieces and place in a 5- to 6-quart (5- to 6-liter) pan. Add broth, vinegar, sugar, ginger, and red pepper flakes. Cover and bring to a boil over high heat; then reduce heat and simmer gently until squash and potatoes are soft enough to mash easily, about 30 minutes. (At this point, you may let cool, then cover and refrigerate for up to 2 days.)

In a small bowl, combine oil, garlic, and 1 tablespoon (15 ml) water. Spread bread cubes on a nonstick 10- by 15-inch (25- by 38-cm) baking sheet; brush evenly with oil

Soups

✳

mixture. Season to taste with salt and pepper. Bake in a 350°F (175°C) oven until croutons are crisp and golden (10 to 12 minutes). If made ahead, let cool completely on baking sheet on a rack; then store airtight for up to 2 days.

In a food processor or blender, whirl squash mixture, a portion at a time, until smoothly puréed. Return purée to pan and stir often over medium-high heat until steaming. Ladle soup into bowls; top with croutons. Makes 6 to 8 servings.

Per serving: *216 calories (15% calories from fat), 4 g total fat, 0.4 g saturated fat, 0 mg cholesterol, 1,088 mg sodium, 45 g carbohydrates, 4 g fiber, 3 g protein, 76 mg calcium, 2 mg iron*

Mushroom Barley Soup

Preparation time: *20 minutes*
Cooking time: *1 to 1¼ hours*

1 tablespoon (15 ml) salad oil or olive oil

1 pound (455 g) mushrooms, thinly sliced

1 large onion, chopped

2 medium-size carrots (about 8 oz./230 g *total*), thinly sliced

10 cups (2.4 liters) vegetable broth

1 cup (200 g) pearl barley, rinsed and drained

1 tablespoon finely chopped fresh oregano or 1 teaspoon dried oregano

8 ounces (230 g) red or green Swiss chard

Pepper

Heat oil in a 5- to 6-quart (5- to 6-liter) pan over medium-high heat. Add mushrooms, onion, and carrots. Cook, stirring often, until vegetables are soft and almost all liquid has evaporated (about 25 minutes). Add broth, barley, and oregano. Bring to a boil over high heat; then reduce heat, cover, and simmer until barley is tender to bite (about 30 minutes).

Meanwhile, trim and discard discolored stem ends from chard. Rinse chard and drain well; then coarsely chop leaves and stems.

Stir chard into soup and simmer, uncovered, until leaves are limp and bright green (5 to 10 minutes). Ladle soup into bowls; season to taste with pepper. Makes 6 to 8 servings.

Per serving: *196 calories (18% calories from fat), 4 g total fat, 0.3 g saturated fat, 0 mg cholesterol, 1,512 mg sodium, 37 g carbohydrates, 7 g fiber, 5 g protein, 47 mg calcium, 2 mg iron*

Sherried Lentil Bisque

Preparation time: *30 minutes*
Cooking time: *About 55 minutes*

2	packages (about 12 oz./340 g *each*, about 3½ cups *total*) lentils
11	cups (2.6 liters) vegetable broth
3	cups (369 g) chopped celery
3	cups (390 g) chopped carrots
3	large onions, chopped
1	small red or green bell pepper (about 4 oz./115 g), seeded and finely chopped
1	medium-size zucchini (about 6 oz./170 g), finely chopped
3	tablespoons (45 ml) dry sherry
4½	teaspoons (23 ml) cream sherry
1	cup reduced-fat sour cream Thinly sliced green onions Salt and pepper

Sort through lentils, discarding any debris. Rinse and drain lentils; place in an 8- to 10-quart (8- to 10-liter) pan and add broth, celery, carrots, chopped onions, bell pepper, and zucchini. Bring to a boil over high heat; then reduce heat, cover, and simmer until lentils are very soft to bite (about 50 minutes).

In a food processor or blender, whirl hot lentil mixture, a portion at a time, until smoothly puréed. Return purée to pan and stir in dry sherry and cream sherry. If made ahead, let cool; then cover and refrigerate until next day.

To serve, stir soup often over medium-high heat until steaming; ladle into bowls. Top with sour cream and green onions; season to taste with salt and pepper. Makes 12 servings.

Per serving: 293 calories (13% calories from fat), 4 g total fat, 1 g saturated fat, 7 mg cholesterol, 959 mg sodium, 47 g carbohydrates, 9 g fiber, 19 g protein, 63 mg calcium, 6 mg iron

Black & White Bean Soup

Preparation time: *25 minutes*
Cooking time: *About 20 minutes*

1	large onion, chopped
1	clove garlic, peeled and sliced
3½	cups (830 ml) vegetable broth
⅓	cup (55 g) oil-packed dried tomatoes, drained and finely chopped
4	green onions, thinly sliced
¼	cup (60 ml) dry sherry
2	cans (about 15 oz./425 g *each*) black beans, drained and rinsed well
2	cans (about 15 oz./425 g *each*) cannellini (white kidney beans), drained and rinsed Slivered green onions (optional)

In a 5- to 6-quart (5- to 6-liter) pan, combine chopped onion, garlic, and ½ cup (120 ml) water. Cook over medium-high heat, stirring often, until liquid evaporates and browned bits stick to pan bottom (about 10 minutes). To deglaze pan, add 2 tablespoons (30 ml) of the broth, stirring to loosen browned bits from pan; continue to cook until browned bits form again. Repeat deglazing step, using 2 tablespoons (30 ml) more broth. Then stir in ½ cup (120 ml) more broth and pour mixture into a food processor or blender.

In same pan, combine tomatoes and sliced green onions. Cook over high heat, stirring, until onions are wilted (about 2 minutes). Add sherry and stir until liquid has evaporated. Remove from heat.

To onion mixture in food processor, add black beans. Whirl, gradually adding 1¼ cups (300 ml) of the broth, until smoothly puréed. Pour into a 3- to 4-quart (2.8- to 3.8-liter) pan.

Rinse processor; add cannellini and whirl until smoothly puréed, gradually adding remaining 1½ cups (360 ml) broth. Stir puréed cannellini into pan with tomato mixture. Place both pans of soup over medium-high heat and cook, stirring often, until steaming.

To serve, pour soup into 6 wide 1½- to 2-cup (360- to 470-ml) bowls as follows. From pans (or from 2 lipped containers such as 4-cup/950-ml pitchers, which are easier to handle), pour soups simultaneously into opposite sides of each bowl so that soups flow together but do not mix. Garnish with slivered green onions, if desired. Makes 6 servings.

Per serving: 283 calories (25% calories from fat), 8 g total fat, 0.9 g saturated fat, 0 mg cholesterol, 996 mg sodium, 38 g carbohydrates, 11 g fiber, 14 g protein, 80 mg calcium, 4 mg iron

Creamy Beet Borscht

Preparation time: *10 minutes*

2	cans (about 15 oz./425 g *each*) pickled beets About 4 cups (950 ml) plain nonfat yogurt
1	cup (240 ml) vegetable broth Dill sprigs Pepper

Drain beets, reserving 1½ cups (360 ml) of the liquid. In a large bowl, combine beets, reserved liquid, 4 cups (950 ml) of the yogurt, and broth. In a food processor or blender, whirl beet mixture, about a third at a time, until smoothly puréed. If made ahead, cover and refrigerate until next day.

Serve borscht cool or cold. To serve, ladle into wide bowls. Add yogurt to taste and garnish with dill sprigs. Season to taste with pepper. Makes 6 to 8 servings.

Per serving: 113 calories (4% calories from fat), 0.5 g total fat, 0.2 g saturated fat, 3 mg cholesterol, 582 mg sodium, 19 g carbohydrates, 1 g fiber, 8 g protein, 276 mg calcium, 1 mg iron

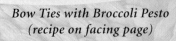

*Bow Ties with Broccoli Pesto
(recipe on facing page)*

Bow Ties with Broccoli Pesto *(Pictured on facing page)*

1	pound (455 g) broccoli flowerets (about 7 cups)
2	or 3 cloves garlic, minced or pressed
½	cup (40 g) grated Parmesan cheese
3	tablespoons (45 ml) olive oil
1½	teaspoons Oriental sesame oil
½	teaspoon salt
12	ounces (340 g) dried pasta bow ties (farfalle)
1	to 2 tablespoons (15 to 30 ml) seasoned rice vinegar (or 1 to 2 tablespoons/15 to 30 ml distilled white vinegar plus ½ to 1 teaspoon sugar)
1	small tomato (about 4 oz./115 g), chopped

Classic pesto sauce is made with fresh basil, but this version is based on bright broccoli flowerets instead. Accented with sesame oil and rice vinegar, the smooth green sauce is delicious over any kind of pasta; we use bow ties here.

Preparation time: 15 minutes   **Cooking time:** About 20 minutes

1 In a 4- to 5-quart (3.8- to 5-liter) pan, bring 8 cups (1.9 liters) water to a boil over medium-high heat. Stir in broccoli and cook until just tender to bite (about 7 minutes). Immediately drain broccoli, immerse in ice water until cool, and drain again. In a food processor or blender, combine a third of the broccoli with garlic, cheese, olive oil, sesame oil, salt, and 3 tablespoons (45 ml) water. Whirl until smooth. Scrape down sides of container, add half the remaining broccoli, and whirl until smooth again. Add remaining broccoli; whirl until smooth. Set aside.

2 In a 5- to 6-quart (5- to 6-liter) pan, bring about 3 quarts (2.8 liters) water to a boil over medium-high heat; stir in pasta and cook until just tender to bite, 8 to 10 minutes. (Or cook pasta according to package directions.)

3 Drain pasta well. Transfer to a large serving bowl and stir in vinegar. Add pesto and mix gently but thoroughly. Garnish with tomato and serve immediately. Makes 4 servings.

Per serving: *510 calories (29% calories from fat), 17 g total fat, 4 g saturated fat, 8 mg cholesterol, 604 mg sodium, 73 g carbohydrates, 6 g fiber, 19 g protein, 204 mg calcium, 4 mg iron*

Pasta with Lentils & Oranges

4	or 5 large oranges (2 to 2½ lbs./905 g to 1.15 kg *total*)
8	large butter lettuce leaves, rinsed and crisped
1	tablespoon grated orange peel
¾	cup (180 ml) fresh orange juice
3	tablespoons chopped fresh basil or 1 tablespoon dried basil
3	tablespoons (45 ml) white wine vinegar
1	tablespoon (15 ml) *each* honey and Dijon mustard
2	to 3 cloves garlic, minced or pressed
1½	teaspoons ground cumin
⅛	teaspoon crushed red pepper flakes (or to taste)
2	cups (470 ml) vegetable broth
¾	cup (150 g) lentils
12	ounces (340 g) dried radiatorre or fusilli
	Basil sprigs

Refreshing oranges lend flavor and color to this combination of tender lentils and fanciful pasta shapes. To complete the presentation, serve the dish atop a bed of butter lettuce leaves and orange slices.

Preparation time: 20 minutes   **Cooking time:** About 30 minutes

1 Cut peel and all white membrane from oranges. Coarsely chop one of the oranges and set aside. Thinly slice remaining 3 or 4 oranges crosswise. Arrange lettuce leaves in a wide, shallow bowl or on a rimmed platter. Top with orange slices; cover and set aside.

2 In a small bowl, stir together chopped orange, orange peel, orange juice, 2 tablespoons of the chopped basil (or 2 teaspoons of the dried basil), vinegar, honey, mustard, garlic, cumin, and red pepper flakes. Beat until blended; set aside.

3 In a 1½- to 2-quart (1.4- to 1.9-liter) pan, bring broth to a boil over medium-high heat. Sort through lentils, discarding any debris; rinse, drain, and add to pan along with remaining 1 tablespoon chopped basil (or 1 teaspoon dried basil). Reduce heat, cover, and simmer until lentils are tender to bite (about 25 minutes).

4 Meanwhile, in a 5- to 6-quart (5- to 6-liter) pan, bring about 3 quarts (2.8 liters) water to a boil over medium-high heat; stir in pasta and cook until just until tender to bite, 8 to 10 minutes. (Or cook pasta according to package directions.)

5 Drain pasta well; if necessary, drain lentils well. Transfer pasta and lentils to a large bowl. Add orange dressing and mix gently but thoroughly. Spoon pasta over orange slices. Garnish with basil sprigs. Makes 4 servings.

Per serving: *563 calories (4% calories from fat), 3 g total fat, 0.3 g saturated fat, 0 mg cholesterol, 601 mg sodium, 115 g carbohydrates, 10 g fiber, 21 g protein, 145 mg calcium, 7 mg iron*

Peanut Pasta & Tofu

¼ cup (60 ml) seasoned rice vinegar (or ¼ cup/60 ml distilled white vinegar plus 2 teaspoons sugar)

3 tablespoons (45 ml) Oriental sesame oil

1 tablespoon (15 ml) reduced-sodium soy sauce

1 teaspoon sugar

1 package (about 14 oz./400 g) regular tofu, rinsed, drained, and cut into ½-inch (1-cm) cubes

12 ounces (340 g) dried penne

2 cups (170 g) Chinese pea pods (also called snow or sugar peas), ends and strings removed

2 cloves garlic, minced

½ cup (120 ml) plum jam

¼ cup (60 ml) crunchy peanut butter

⅛ teaspoon ground ginger

⅓ cup (15 g) cilantro leaves

¼ cup (25 g) sliced green onions

Cilantro sprigs

Crushed red pepper flakes

Asian-style peanut sauce is great with all sorts of foods, from pork and beef to chicken and noodles. Here, it's tossed with chunky pasta tubes and marinated tofu.

Preparation time: 20 minutes   **Cooking time:** About 20 minutes

1 In a shallow bowl, beat vinegar, 1 tablespoon (15 ml) of the oil, soy sauce, and sugar until blended. Add tofu and mix gently. Set aside; stir occasionally.

2 In a 5- to 6-quart (5- to 6-liter) pan, bring about 3 quarts (2.8 liters) water to a boil over medium-high heat; stir in pasta and cook until almost tender to bite, 7 to 9 minutes. (Or cook pasta according to package directions, cooking for a little less than the recommended time.) Add pea pods to boiling water with pasta and cook for 1 more minute. Drain pasta mixture, rinse with hot water, and drain well again; keep warm.

3 With a slotted spoon, transfer tofu to a large, shallow serving bowl; reserve marinade from tofu.

4 In pan used to cook pasta, heat remaining 2 tablespoons (30 ml) oil over medium heat. Add garlic and cook, stirring, just until fragrant (about 30 seconds; do not scorch). Add jam, peanut butter, marinade from tofu, and ginger. Cook, whisking, just until sauce is smooth and well blended. Remove pan from heat and add pasta mixture, cilantro leaves, and onions. Mix gently but thoroughly. Transfer pasta to bowl with tofu and mix very gently. Garnish with cilantro sprigs. Serve at once; season to taste with red pepper flakes. Makes 4 servings.

Per serving: *714 calories (30% calories from fat), 25 g total fat, 4 g saturated fat, 0 mg cholesterol, 558 mg sodium, 103 g carbohydrates, 6 g fiber, 25 g protein, 162 mg calcium, 10 mg iron*

Ravioli with Gorgonzola

2 packages (about 9 oz./255 g *each*) fresh low-fat or regular cheese-filled ravioli

¼ cup (45 g) finely chopped onion

2 cloves garlic, minced or pressed

4 teaspoons cornstarch

1 cup (240 ml) nonfat milk

½ cup (120 ml) *each* half-and-half and vegetable broth

2 ounces (55 g) Gorgonzola or other blue-veined cheese, crumbled

¼ teaspoon *each* dried thyme, marjoram, and rubbed sage

⅛ teaspoon ground nutmeg

1 teaspoon dry sherry (or to taste)

Finely shredded lemon peel

Salt and pepper

Piquant Gorgonzola cheese and a hint of sherry give this creamy ravioli its sprightly character.

Preparation time: 15 minutes   **Cooking time:** About 25 minutes

1 In a 6- to 8-quart (6- to 8-liter) pan, bring about 4 quarts (3.8 liters) water to a boil over medium-high heat. Stir in ravioli, separating any that are stuck together; reduce heat and boil gently, stirring occasionally, until pasta is just tender to bite, 4 to 6 minutes. (Or cook pasta according to package directions.) Drain well, return to pan, and keep warm.

2 While pasta is cooking, combine onion, garlic, and 1 tablespoon (15 ml) water in a wide nonstick frying pan. Cook over medium-high heat, stirring often, until onion is soft (3 to 4 minutes); add water, 1 tablespoon (15 ml) at a time, if pan appears dry. Remove from heat.

3 Smoothly blend cornstarch with 2 tablespoons (30 ml) of the milk. Add cornstarch mixture, remaining milk, half-and-half, and broth to pan. Return to medium-high heat and bring to a boil, stirring. Reduce heat to low and add cheese, thyme, marjoram, sage, and nutmeg; stir until cheese is melted. Remove pan from heat and stir in sherry.

4 Spoon sauce over pasta; mix gently. Spoon pasta onto individual plates; sprinkle with lemon peel. Season to taste with salt and pepper. Makes 6 servings.

Per serving: *315 calories (29% calories from fat), 10 g total fat, 6 g saturated fat, 69 mg cholesterol, 545 mg sodium, 40 g carbohydrates, 2 g fiber, 15 g protein, 270 mg calcium, 2 mg iron*

Sicilian Pasta Timbale

Marinara Sauce:

1   teaspoon olive oil

3   cloves garlic, minced or
     pressed

1   large can (about 28 oz./795 g)
     tomato purée

¼   cup (10 g) chopped fresh basil
     or 2 tablespoons dried basil
     Salt

Pasta Timbale:

2   small eggplants (about
     1 lb./455 g *each*)

2   teaspoons salt

4   to 6 teaspoons (20 to 30 ml)
     olive oil

1   pound (455 g) dried salad
     macaroni

2   cups (about 8 oz./230 g)
     shredded provolone cheese

½   cup (40 g) grated Romano
     cheese

     About 1 teaspoon butter or
     margarine, at room
     temperature

2   tablespoons fine dry bread
     crumbs

Garnish:

     Basil sprigs

Served in wedges, this hearty timbale is a grand meatless main dish. To make it, you layer roasted eggplant slices with a savory mixture of cooked macaroni, marinara sauce, herbs, and cheese; then bake.

Preparation time: 20 minutes, plus 15 minutes for eggplant to stand   **Cooking time:** About 1 hour

1 Heat the 1 teaspoon oil in a 3- to 4-quart (2.8- to 3.8-liter) pan over medium heat. Add garlic and cook, stirring, just until fragrant (about 30 seconds; do not scorch). Add tomato purée and chopped basil. Bring to a boil; then reduce heat and simmer, uncovered, stirring occasionally, until sauce is reduced to about 3 cups/710 ml (about 20 minutes). Season to taste with salt; set aside.

2 While sauce is simmering, cut eggplants lengthwise into ¼-inch (6-mm) slices; sprinkle with the 2 teaspoons salt. Let stand for 15 minutes; then rinse well and pat dry. Coat 2 or 3 shallow 10- by 15-inch (25- by 38-cm) baking pans with oil, using 2 teaspoons oil per pan. Turn eggplant slices in oil to coat both sides; arrange in a single layer. Bake in a 425°F (220°C) oven until eggplant is browned and soft when pressed (about 25 minutes; remove pieces as they brown).

3 In a 6- to 8-quart (6- to 8-liter) pan, bring about 4 quarts (3.8 liters) water to a boil over medium-high heat; stir in pasta and cook until just barely tender to bite, 6 to 8 minutes. (Or cook pasta according to package directions, cooking slightly less than time recommended.) Drain pasta well and mix with provolone cheese, 2 cups (470 ml) of the marinara sauce, and 6 tablespoons (30 g) of the Romano cheese.

4 Butter sides and bottom of a 9-inch (23-cm) cheesecake pan with a removable rim. Dust pan with bread crumbs. Arrange a third of the eggplant slices in pan, overlapping them to cover bottom of pan. Cover with half the pasta mixture. Add a layer of half the remaining eggplant, then evenly top with remaining pasta mixture. Top evenly with remaining eggplant. Press down gently to compact layers and to make timbale level. Sprinkle with remaining 2 tablespoons Romano cheese. (At this point, you may cover and refrigerate until next day.)

5 Bake, uncovered, in a 350°F (175°C) oven until hot in center, about 30 minutes. (If refrigerated, bake, covered, for 30 minutes; then uncover and continue to bake until hot in center, about 30 more minutes.) Let stand for about 5 minutes before serving.

6 Meanwhile, pour remaining marinara sauce into a 1- to 1½-quart (950-ml to 1.4-liter) pan; stir over medium heat until steaming. Transfer to a small pitcher or sauce boat. With a knife, cut around edge of timbale to release; remove pan rim. Garnish timbale with basil sprigs. Cut into wedges; serve with hot marinara sauce. Makes 6 to 8 servings.

Per serving: 503 calories (27% calories from fat), 15 g total fat, 7 g saturated fat, 30 mg cholesterol, 994 mg sodium, 71 g carbohydrates, 6 g fiber, 22 g protein, 416 mg calcium, 5 mg iron

Pasta Pie *(Pictured on facing page)*

Pasta Pie:

½ cup (120 ml) nonfat milk

1 teaspoon cornstarch

2 large eggs

6 large egg whites

¾ cup (85 g) shredded part-skim mozzarella cheese

¼ cup (20 g) grated Parmesan cheese

2 tablespoons chopped fresh oregano or 1½ teaspoons dried oregano

2 cloves garlic, minced or pressed

¼ teaspoon salt

⅛ teaspoon crushed red pepper flakes

3 cups (390 g) cold cooked spaghetti

1 teaspoon salad oil

Tomato Cream Sauce:

1 large can (about 28 oz./795 g) diced tomatoes

½ cup (120 ml) reduced-fat sour cream

2 or 3 cloves garlic, peeled

2 teaspoons chopped fresh thyme or ½ teaspoon dried thyme

1 teaspoon sugar (or to taste)
   Salt and pepper

Garnish:

Oregano sprigs and fresh oregano leaves

Pasta lovers will enjoy this light and savory pie, made from cooked spaghetti, eggs, and two kinds of cheese. A creamy tomato sauce enhances the dish.

Preparation time: 15 minutes   **Cooking time:** About 30 minutes

1 In a large bowl, combine milk and cornstarch; beat until smoothly blended. Add eggs and egg whites and beat well. Stir in mozzarella cheese, Parmesan cheese, chopped oregano, minced garlic, the ¼ teaspoon salt, and red pepper flakes. Add pasta to egg mixture; lift with 2 forks to mix well. Set aside.

2 Place a 9-inch-round (23-cm-round) baking pan (do not use a nonstick pan) in oven while it heats to 500°F (260°C). When pan is hot (after about 5 minutes), carefully remove it from oven and pour in oil, tilting pan to coat. Mix pasta mixture again; then transfer to pan. Bake on lowest rack of oven until top of pie is golden and center feels firm when lightly pressed (about 25 minutes).

3 Meanwhile, pour tomatoes and their liquid into a food processor or blender. Add sour cream, peeled garlic, thyme, and sugar; whirl until smoothly puréed. Season to taste with salt and pepper; set aside. Use at room temperature.

4 When pie is done, spread about ¾ cup (180 ml) of the sauce on each of 4 individual plates. Cut pie into 4 wedges; place one wedge atop sauce on each plate. Garnish with oregano sprigs and leaves. Offer remaining sauce to drizzle over pie. Makes 4 servings.

Per serving: 411 calories (30% calories from fat), 14 g total fat, 6 g saturated fat, 133 mg cholesterol, 782 mg sodium, 47 g carbohydrates, 3 g fiber, 26 g protein, 340 mg calcium, 4 mg iron

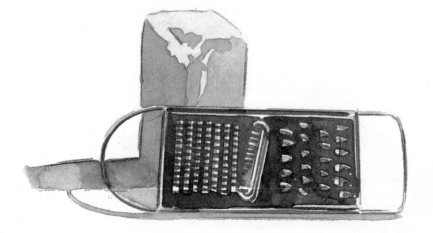

Pasta Pie
(recipe on facing page)

Couscous with Berries & Shrimp

Preparation time: *15 minutes, plus about 10 minutes for couscous to cool*
Cooking time: *About 5 minutes*

1   package (about 10 oz./ 285 g) couscous
1   small cucumber (about 8 oz./230 g)
1   cup (40 g) firmly packed fresh mint leaves
½   cup (120 ml) lemon juice
2   tablespoons (30 ml) olive oil
    About ½ teaspoon honey (or to taste)
1   cup (145 g) fresh blueberries or other fresh berries
    Salt and pepper
4   to 8 large butter lettuce leaves, rinsed and crisped
6   to 8 ounces (170 to 230 g) small cooked shrimp
    Lemon wedges and mint sprigs

In a 2½- to 3-quart (2.4- to 2.8-liter) pan, bring 2¼ cups (530 ml) water to a boil over medium-high heat. Stir in couscous; cover, remove from heat, and let stand until liquid has been absorbed (about 5 minutes). Then transfer couscous to a large bowl and let stand until cool (about 10 minutes), fluffing often with a fork.

Meanwhile, peel, halve, and seed cucumber; thinly slice halves and set aside. Finely chop mint leaves, place in a small bowl, and mix in lemon juice, oil, and honey. Add cucumber and blueberries to couscous; then add mint dressing and mix gently but thoroughly. Season to taste with salt and pepper.

Line each of 4 individual plates with 1 or 2 lettuce leaves. Mound couscous mixture in center of each plate; top with shrimp. Garnish

Almost Vegetarian Pasta
✳

with lemon wedges and mint sprigs.
Makes 4 servings.

Per serving: 419 calories (18% calories from fat), 8 g total fat, 1 g saturated fat, 97 mg cholesterol, 129 mg sodium, 66 g carbohydrates, 4 g fiber, 21 g protein, 66 mg calcium, 3 mg iron

✳

Spinach Tortellini with Spinach & Pears

Preparation time: *25 minutes*
Cooking time: *About 25 minutes*

30 to 40 large fresh whole spinach leaves, rinsed and crisped
5   large red pears (about 2½ lbs./1.15 kg *total*)
1   tablespoon (15 ml) lemon juice
1   to 2 ounces (30 to 55 g) prosciutto, cut into thin strips about 1 inch (2.5 cm) long
1   package (about 10 oz./285 g) fresh spinach, stems and any yellow or wilted leaves discarded, remaining leaves rinsed and drained
1   tablespoon butter or margarine
¼   cup (60 ml) half-and-half
½   to 1 teaspoon honey
    About ¼ teaspoon salt (or to taste)
    About ¹⁄₁₆ teaspoon ground nutmeg (or to taste)
1   package (about 9 oz./255 g) fresh cheese-filled spinach tortellini
    Lemon wedges

Divide whole spinach leaves among 4 individual plates; set aside. Peel, core, and thinly slice one of the pears. Place pear slices in a large bowl, add lemon juice, and turn to coat. With a slotted spoon, transfer pear slices to a small bowl and set aside; reserve lemon juice in large bowl.

Core and slice remaining pears (do not peel); add to juice in large bowl and turn to coat. Arrange pear slices over one side of each spinach-lined plate; cover and set aside. Discard any remaining lemon juice.

In a wide nonstick frying pan, stir prosciutto over medium-high heat just until crisp (1 to 2 minutes). Remove from pan with a slotted spoon; set aside. Add as much of the packaged spinach as pan will hold. Reduce heat to medium and cook, stirring, just until wilted; add water, 1 tablespoon (15 ml) at a time, if pan appears dry. Transfer cooked spinach to a bowl; repeat to cook remaining spinach. With the back of a wooden spoon, press against spinach to remove excess liquid; discard as much liquid as possible. Keep spinach warm.

Melt butter in frying pan and add reserved sliced peeled pears. Sauté until almost tender when pierced (3 to 5 minutes). Working quickly, transfer pears and their juices to a blender or food processor; add cooked spinach and whirl until coarsely puréed. Add half-and-half, honey, salt, and nutmeg. Whirl until smooth; keep warm.

In a 5- to 6-quart (5- to 6-liter) pan, bring about 3 quarts (2.8 liters) water to a boil over medium-high heat. Stir in tortellini, separating any that are stuck together, and cook until just tender to bite, about 7 minutes. (Or cook pasta according to package directions.)

Drain pasta well and transfer to a large bowl. Add spinach-pear purée and mix gently but thoroughly. Spoon pasta atop spinach leaves alongside pears on plates. Sprinkle prosciutto over pasta and serve immediately. Offer lemon wedges to squeeze over pasta to taste. Makes 4 servings.

Per serving: 430 calories (23% calories from fat), 12 g total fat, 6 g saturated fat, 62 mg cholesterol, 716 mg sodium, 73 g carbohydrates, 11 g fiber, 16 g protein, 236 mg calcium, 4 mg iron

---

✳

Pasta with Shrimp & Shiitake Mushrooms

Preparation time: *20 minutes*
Cooking time: *About 15 minutes*

---

2   cups (about 2 oz./55 g) dried shiitake mushrooms
8   ounces (230 g) dried capellini
2   teaspoons Oriental sesame oil
6   tablespoons (90 ml) oyster sauce or reduced-sodium soy sauce
1   tablespoon (15 ml) salad oil
12 ounces (340 g) medium-size raw shrimp (31 to 35 per lb.), shelled and deveined
1   tablespoon finely chopped fresh ginger
3   green onions, thinly sliced

Place mushrooms in a medium-size bowl and add enough boiling water to cover; let stand until mushrooms are softened (about 10 minutes). Squeeze mushrooms dry. Cut off and discard stems. Slice caps into strips about ¼ inch (6 mm) thick.

In a 4- to 5-quart (3.8- to 5-liter) pan, bring about 8 cups (1.9 liters) water to a boil over medium-high heat; stir in pasta and cook until just tender to bite, about 3 minutes. (Or cook according to package directions.) Drain pasta, rinse with hot water, and drain well again. Then return to pan, add sesame oil and 3 tablespoons (45 ml) of the oyster sauce, and lift with 2 forks to mix. Keep warm.

Heat salad oil in a wide nonstick frying pan over medium-high heat. Add mushrooms, shrimp, and ginger. Cook, stirring often, until shrimp are just opaque in center; cut to test (about 5 minutes). Add onions and remaining 3 tablespoons (45 ml) oyster sauce; mix gently but thoroughly. Pour noodles into a wide bowl; pour shrimp mixture over noodles. Makes 4 servings.

Per serving: 409 calories (17% calories from fat), 8 g total fat, 1 g saturated fat, 105 mg cholesterol, 1,181 mg sodium, 64 g carbohydrates, 2 g fiber, 25 g protein, 59 mg calcium, 5 mg iron

✳

Chinese Black Bean, Noodle & Chicken Salad

Preparation time: *20 minutes*
Cooking time: *About 35 minutes*

---

2   small boneless, skinless chicken breast halves (about 8 oz./230 g *total*)
½   cup (120 ml) seasoned rice vinegar (or ½ cup/120 ml distilled white vinegar plus 4 teaspoons sugar)
6   tablespoons (90 ml) lime juice
1   tablespoon (15 ml) Oriental sesame oil
    About 1 tablespoon (15 ml) reduced-sodium soy sauce
2   teaspoons sugar
    About ⅛ teaspoon crushed red pepper flakes (or to taste)
4   cups (about 4 oz./115 g) mixed salad greens, rinsed and crisped
1   package (about 12 oz./340 g) fresh thin Chinese-style noodles or 12 ounces (340 g) dried capellini

1   can (about 15 oz./425 g) black beans, drained and rinsed well
½   cup (50 g) thinly sliced green onions
½   cup (20 g) cilantro leaves
¼   cup (36 g) chopped salted roasted peanuts
    Lime wedges and cilantro sprigs

Rinse chicken and pat dry. In a 5- to 6-quart (5- to 6-liter) pan with a tight-fitting lid, bring 3 quarts (2.8 liters) water to a rolling boil over high heat. Remove pan from heat and immediately add chicken. Cover pan tightly and let stand until meat in thickest part is no longer pink; cut to test (15 to 20 minutes; do not uncover until ready to test). If chicken is not done, return it to hot water, cover, and steep for 2 to 3 more minutes.

Meanwhile, in a large bowl, combine 6 tablespoons (90 ml) of the vinegar, lime juice, oil, soy sauce, sugar, and red pepper flakes; set aside. In another bowl, mix greens and remaining 2 tablespoons (30 ml) vinegar. Arrange greens on 4 individual plates; set aside.

When chicken is done, lift it from pan with a slotted spoon and let stand just until cool enough to handle. Then shred chicken and add to bowl with vinegar mixture; set aside.

In a 5- to 6-quart (5- to 6-liter) pan, bring about 3 quarts (2.8 liters) water to a boil over medium-high heat; stir in pasta and cook until just tender to bite (4 to 6 minutes for fresh pasta, about 3 minutes for dried). Or cook pasta according to package directions.

Drain pasta well and transfer to bowl with chicken. Add beans, onions, and cilantro leaves; mix gently but thoroughly. Spoon pasta over greens. Garnish with peanuts, lime wedges, and cilantro sprigs. Serve at once. Makes 4 servings.

Per serving: 503 calories (20% calories from fat), 11 g total fat, 2 g saturated fat, 95 mg cholesterol, 986 mg sodium, 71 g carbohydrates, 6 g fiber, 30 g protein, 88 mg calcium, 6 mg iron

Fruited Basmati Pilaf
(recipe on page 40)

WHOLE GRAINS

✳

*S*alads, pilaf, gnocchi, creamy casseroles, risotto—you'll find them all here. Most of these entrées feature familiar ingredients like rice, polenta, and bulgur; a few are based on grains you may not know so well, such as quinoa and wheat berries. Many of our recipes gain special appeal from their seasonings and presentation. Who could resist Fruited Basmati Pilaf with succulent mangoes and crunchy macadamia nuts, or refreshingly cool Bulgur Tabbouleh Salad, lively with mint and lemon?

✳

Fruited Basmati Pilaf *(Pictured on page 38)*

1   cup (200 g) orange lentils
2   teaspoons butter or margarine
1   cup (185 g) basmati or long-grain white rice
4¼ cups (1 liter) vegetable broth
1   can (about 12 oz./360 ml) mango or apricot nectar
⅛   teaspoon ground coriander
¼   cup (35 g) coarsely chopped dried apricots
4   large mangoes (about 3 lbs./1.35 kg *total*)
3   tablespoons (45 ml) lime juice
½   cup (75 g) dried currants or raisins
⅓   cup (35 g) thinly sliced green onion tops
¾   cup (108 g) coarsely chopped salted roasted macadamia nuts or peanuts
    Lime wedges or slices

Aromatic basmati rice simmers in mango nectar for an especially fragrant pilaf. The dish is pretty to look at, too—it's dotted with dried apricots, currants, and bright orange lentils. Look for orange lentils in Indian markets; if you can't find them, use the familiar brown, yellow, or green variety.

Preparation time: 20 minutes   **Cooking time:** About 35 minutes

1   Sort through lentils, discarding any debris. Rinse and drain lentils; then set aside.

2   Melt butter in a 4- to 5-quart (3.8- to 5-liter) pan over medium heat. Add rice and cook, stirring often, until opaque (about 3 minutes). Add broth, mango nectar, and coriander. Increase heat to medium-high and bring mixture just to a boil. Stir in lentils and apricots; then reduce heat, cover, and simmer until liquid has been absorbed and both rice and lentils are tender to bite (about 25 minutes). If any cooking liquid remains, drain and discard it.

3   While rice mixture is simmering, peel mangoes and slice fruit from pits into a large bowl. Add lime juice and mix gently to coat. Arrange mangoes decoratively around edge of a rimmed platter; cover and set aside.

4   Remove rice mixture from heat; stir in currants and onions. Spoon pilaf into center of platter; sprinkle macadamia nuts over mangoes and pilaf. Garnish with lime wedges. Makes 6 servings.

Per serving: *519 calories (25% calories from fat), 16 g total fat, 3 g saturated fat, 3 mg cholesterol, 745 mg sodium, 91 g carbohydrates, 6 g fiber, 14 g protein, 63 mg calcium, 4 mg iron*

Bulgur Tabbouleh Salad

2   cups (350 g) bulgur
1½   cups (60 g) firmly packed fresh mint leaves
1   can (about 15 oz./425 g) garbanzo beans, drained and rinsed
     About ½ cup (120 ml) lemon juice (or to taste)
2   tablespoons (30 ml) olive oil
     Salt and pepper
     About 8 large butter lettuce leaves, rinsed and crisped
2   large firm-ripe tomatoes (about 1 lb./455 g *total*), thinly sliced
4   ounces (115 g) feta cheese, crumbled
     Mint sprigs and lemon slices

Refreshing and easy to prepare, this sprightly salad is perfect for warm summer days. Serve it with assorted fresh fruit and a crusty loaf of bread.

Preparation time: 15 minutes, plus about 1 hour for bulgur to stand and at least 30 minutes for salad to chill

1   In a deep bowl, mix bulgur and 2 cups (470 ml) cold water. Let stand until grain is tender to bite and water has been absorbed (about 1 hour), stirring occasionally.

2   Finely chop mint leaves and add to bulgur along with beans, lemon juice, and oil. Mix well; season to taste with salt and pepper. Cover and refrigerate until cool (at least 30 minutes) or for up to 4 hours.

3   Line a platter with lettuce leaves. Arrange tomatoes around edge of platter; mound tabbouleh in center and sprinkle with cheese. Garnish with mint sprigs and lemon slices. Makes 4 servings.

Per serving: *486 calories (28% calories from fat), 16 g total fat, 5 g saturated fat, 25 mg cholesterol, 463 mg sodium, 74 g carbohydrates, 17 g fiber, 18 g protein, 219 mg calcium, 5 mg iron*

Warm Wild Rice & Asparagus Salad

1 cup (170 g) wild rice, rinsed and drained

1 cup (200 g) lentils

1 pound (455 g) mushrooms, thinly sliced

1 large onion, chopped

About 2½ cups (590 ml) vegetable broth

1 pound (455 g) slender asparagus

3 tablespoons (45 ml) balsamic vinegar

1 tablespoon (15 ml) olive oil

½ cup (40 g) grated Parmesan cheese

Balsamic vinegar adds a sweet-tart accent to a warm salad of wild rice, lentils, mushrooms, and tender-crisp fresh asparagus.

Preparation time: 15 minutes   **Cooking time:** About 1 hour and 20 minutes

1 In a 5- to 6-quart (5- to 6-liter) pan, combine rice and 8 cups (1.9 liters) water. Bring to a boil over high heat; then reduce heat, cover, and simmer for 30 minutes. Meanwhile, sort through lentils, discarding any debris; rinse lentils, drain, and set aside.

2 Add lentils to rice and continue to simmer until both rice and lentils are tender to bite (about 25 more minutes). Drain and let cool.

3 In a wide nonstick frying pan, combine mushrooms, onion, and ¾ cup (180 ml) of the broth. Cook over medium-high heat, stirring often, until liquid evaporates and browned bits stick to pan bottom (about 10 minutes). To deglaze pan, add ⅓ cup (80 ml) of the broth, stirring to loosen browned bits from pan; continue to cook until browned bits form again. Repeat deglazing step about 3 more times or until vegetables are browned, using ⅓ cup (80 ml) more broth each time.

4 Snap off and discard tough ends of asparagus; thinly slice stalks. Add asparagus and ⅓ cup (80 ml) more broth to mushroom mixture; cook, stirring often, until asparagus is tender-crisp to bite (about 2 minutes).

5 Spoon rice-lentil mixture into a large bowl. Add asparagus mixture, vinegar, and oil; mix gently but thoroughly. Sprinkle with cheese. Makes 8 servings.

Per serving: *236 calories (16% calories from fat), 4 g total fat, 1 g saturated fat, 4 mg cholesterol, 413 mg sodium, 27 g carbohydrates, 6 g fiber, 15 g protein, 106 mg calcium, 4 mg iron*

Barley Casserole

3½ cups (830 ml) vegetable broth

4 cloves garlic, minced or pressed

½ teaspoon dried rosemary, crumbled

¼ teaspoon fennel seeds, crushed

1 cup (200 g) pearl barley, rinsed and drained

1 package (about 10 oz./285 g) frozen baby lima beans, thawed and drained

1 large red or yellow bell pepper (about 8 oz./230 g), seeded and finely chopped

⅓ cup (35 g) thinly sliced green onions

1 tablespoon (15 ml) balsamic vinegar

½ cup (65 g) salted roasted almonds

Rosemary sprigs (optional)

Wholesome, chewy barley seasoned with garlic, rosemary, and fennel mingles with tender lima beans and sweet bell pepper in this one-pan entrée. Garnish the dish with crunchy roasted almonds and aromatic rosemary sprigs.

Preparation time: 20 minutes   **Cooking time:** About 50 minutes

1 In a shallow 1½- to 2-quart (1.4- to 1.9-liter) casserole, combine 3 cups (710 ml) of the broth, garlic, dried rosemary, and fennel seeds. Bake, uncovered, in a 450°F (230°C) oven until mixture comes to a rolling boil (about 20 minutes). Remove from oven and carefully stir in barley. Cover tightly, return to oven, and bake for 10 more minutes. Stir well, cover again, and continue to bake until barley is tender to bite (about 15 more minutes).

2 Stir remaining ½ cup (120 ml) broth, beans, and bell pepper into barley mixture. Bake, uncovered, for 5 more minutes. Remove from oven and stir in onions and vinegar. Spoon barley mixture onto a platter and sprinkle with almonds. Garnish with rosemary sprigs, if desired. Makes 4 servings.

Per serving: *423 calories (27% calories from fat), 13 g total fat, 1 g saturated fat, 0 mg cholesterol, 1,070 mg sodium, 66 g carbohydrates, 14 g fiber, 15 g protein, 102 mg calcium, 4 mg iron*

Polenta Gnocchi with Dried Tomato Chutney *(Pictured on facing page)*

Polenta Gnocchi:

2   cups (470 ml) low-fat (1%) milk

½   cup (120 ml) vegetable broth

1   cup (138 g) polenta or yellow cornmeal

½   teaspoon salt

1   teaspoon chopped fresh sage or ¼ teaspoon ground sage

1   large egg

1   tablespoon butter or margarine

¼   cup (20 g) finely shredded Parmesan cheese

Dried Tomato Chutney:

1   cup (about 2½ oz./70 g) dried tomatoes (not oil-packed)

1   large jar (about 4 oz./115 g) diced pimentos

½   cup (85 g) drained capers

4   cloves garlic, peeled

2   tablespoons chopped fresh basil or 2 teaspoons dried basil

1   tablespoon (15 ml) olive oil

4   teaspoons (20 ml) marsala or port (or to taste)

1   teaspoon Dijon mustard

Garnish:

Sage sprigs

Crunchy on the outside and creamy-textured within, these baked polenta cutouts are enhanced with an unusual chutney based on sweet, richly flavored dried tomatoes, capers, and pimentos.

Preparation time: 30 minutes, plus 15 minutes for polenta to stand   **Cooking time:** About 45 minutes

1   In a 4- to 5-quart (3.8- to 5-liter) pan, bring milk and broth just to a boil over medium-high heat. Stir in polenta, salt, and chopped sage. Reduce heat and simmer, uncovered, stirring often and scraping pan bottom with a long-handled spoon (mixture will spatter), until polenta tastes creamy (about 15 minutes). Remove from heat and stir in egg and butter.

2   Working quickly, brush a 9- by 13-inch (23- by 33-cm) baking pan liberally with water; then spoon polenta into pan and spread to make level. Let stand in pan on a rack for 15 minutes. Then cut polenta diagonally into diamonds, making cuts about 1½ inches (3.5 cm) apart. Carefully arrange polenta pieces, overlapping slightly, in a greased shallow 1½- to 2-quart (1.4- to 1.9-liter) casserole. (At this point, you may let cool, then cover and refrigerate until next day.) Sprinkle with cheese and bake, uncovered, in a 350°F (175°C) oven until hot and tinged with brown (about 20 minutes; about 35 minutes if refrigerated).

3   Meanwhile, place tomatoes in a small bowl and add boiling water to cover. Let stand until soft (about 10 minutes). Drain well; squeeze out excess liquid. Transfer tomatoes to a food processor or blender. Add ⅓ cup (80 ml) water, pimentos, capers, garlic, basil, oil, marsala, and mustard. Whirl until mixture is puréed and has a spoonable consistency. If chutney is too thick, add a little more water. Transfer to a small bowl.

4   Divide gnocchi among 4 individual plates; garnish with sage sprigs. Offer chutney to add to taste. Makes 4 servings.

Per serving: *361 calories (29% calories from fat), 12 g total fat, 5 g saturated fat, 70 mg cholesterol, 1,100 mg sodium, 51 g carbohydrates, 6 g fiber, 14 g protein, 277mg calcium, 4 mg iron*

*Polenta Gnocchi with Dried Tomato Chutney
(recipe on facing page)*

Sweet Corn Risotto

4   medium-size ears corn (*each about 8 inches/20 cm long*)

4   cups (680 g) finely chopped onions

1   tablespoon butter or margarine

2   cups (400 g) arborio or short-grain white rice

8   cups (1.9 liters) vegetable broth

About ½ cup (120 ml) lime juice

2   to 4 tablespoons thinly sliced green onion tops or snipped chives

½   cup (40 g) finely shaved or shredded Parmesan cheese

Salt and pepper

Delicate risotto studded with sweet corn kernels is ideal for a summer evening. Serve it with a platter of sliced red-ripe tomatoes.

Preparation time: 20 minutes   **Cooking time:** About 40 minutes

1   Remove and discard husks and silk from corn. In a shallow pan, hold one ear of corn upright and, with a sharp knife, cut kernels from cob. Then, using blunt edge of knife, scrape juice from cob into pan. Repeat with remaining ears of corn. Discard cobs.

2   In a wide nonstick frying pan, combine 2 cups (340 g) of the chopped onions, butter, and ¼ cup (60 ml) water. Cook over medium-high heat, stirring often, until onions are soft (5 to 10 minutes); add water, 1 tablespoon (15 ml) at a time, if pan appears dry. Add rice and cook, stirring often, until opaque (about 3 minutes). Meanwhile, bring broth to a simmer in a 3- to 4-quart (2.8- to 3.8-liter) pan; keep broth warm.

3   Add ¼ cup (60 ml) of the lime juice and 6 cups (1.4 liters) of the broth to rice mixture. Cook, stirring often, until liquid has been absorbed (about 15 minutes). Add remaining 2 cups (470 ml) broth, corn kernels and juice, and remaining 2 cups (340 g) chopped onions. Cook, stirring often, until rice is tender to bite and mixture is creamy (about 10 minutes).

4   Spoon risotto into wide individual bowls; top with green onions and cheese. Season to taste with salt, pepper, and remaining lime juice. Makes 4 servings.

Per serving: *628 calories (15% calories from fat), 10 g total fat, 4 g saturated fat, 17 mg cholesterol, 2,289 mg sodium, 120 g carbohydrates, 7 g fiber, 17 g protein, 225 mg calcium, 6 mg iron*

Green & Brown Rice

2   cups (370 g) long-grain brown rice

¾   cup (150 g) split peas

4   cups (950 ml) vegetable broth

2½   cups (590 ml) nonfat milk

2   tablespoons drained capers

½   teaspoon ground nutmeg

6   ounces (170 g) fresh spinach, stems and any yellow or wilted leaves discarded, remaining leaves rinsed, drained, and finely chopped

½   cup (40 g) grated Parmesan cheese

⅓   cup (35 g) thinly sliced green onions

Whole fresh spinach leaves, rinsed and crisped

⅓   cup (20 g) finely chopped parsley

½   cup (65 g) salted roasted almonds, chopped

Green split peas, wholesome brown rice, and vivid fresh spinach team up in this colorful entrée. Serve the dish on a bed of whole spinach leaves, with a garnish of crisp salted almonds.

Preparation time: 25 minutes   **Cooking time:** About 1 hour and 10 minutes

1   Spread rice in a shallow 3- to 3½-quart (2.8- to 3.3-liter) casserole, about 9 by 13 inches (23 by 33 cm). Bake in a 350°F (175°C) oven, stirring occasionally, until rice is golden brown (about 25 minutes).

2   Meanwhile, sort through peas, discarding any debris; rinse and drain peas, then set aside.

3   In a 3- to 4-quart (2.8- to 3.8-liter) pan, combine 3½ cups (830 ml) of the broth, milk, capers, and nutmeg. Bring just to a boil over medium-high heat. Leaving casserole in oven, carefully stir broth mixture and peas into rice. Cover tightly and bake until almost all liquid has been absorbed (about 40 minutes); stir after 20 and 30 minutes, covering casserole tightly again each time.

4   Uncover casserole and stir in remaining ½ cup (120 ml) broth, chopped spinach, cheese, and onions; bake, uncovered, for 5 more minutes.

5   To serve, line 6 individual plates with whole spinach leaves. Stir rice mixture and spoon atop spinach; sprinkle with parsley and almonds. Makes 6 servings.

Per serving: *463 calories (24% calories from fat), 13 g total fat, 3 g saturated fat, 7 mg cholesterol, 1,049 mg sodium, 70 g carbohydrates, 6 g fiber, 19 g protein, 309 mg calcium, 3 mg iron*

Quinoa Risotto *(Pictured on page 3)*

1½   cups (255 g) quinoa
1   teaspoon butter or margarine
1   large onion, finely chopped
1   cup (240 ml) vegetable broth
¾   cup (180 ml) nonfat milk
1½   teaspoons chopped fresh sage
     or ½ teaspoon dried rubbed
     sage
8   ounces (230 g) slender
     asparagus
¼   cup (30 g) shredded fontina or
     jack cheese
½   cup (40 g) finely shaved or
     grated Parmesan cheese
     Sage sprigs

Quinoa, often called the "super grain" thanks to its high protein content, replaces the traditional arborio rice as the base for this hearty risotto. You'll find quinoa in natural food stores and well-stocked supermarkets; be sure to rinse it thoroughly before cooking to remove the slightly bitter coating.

Preparation time: 15 minutes   **Cooking time:** About 40 minutes

1 Place quinoa in a fine strainer and rinse thoroughly with cool water; drain well. Then place quinoa in a wide nonstick frying pan and cook over medium heat, stirring often, until darker in color (about 8 minutes). Remove from pan and set aside.

2 Increase heat to medium-high. Melt butter in pan and add onion and 2 tablespoons (30 ml) water. Cook, stirring often, until onion is soft (about 5 minutes); add water, 1 tablespoon (15 ml) at a time, if pan appears dry.

3 To pan, add broth, milk, quinoa, and dried sage (or if using fresh sage, add later, as directed). Bring just to a boil, stirring often. Reduce heat and simmer, uncovered, stirring occasionally, until quinoa is almost tender to bite (about 10 minutes). Meanwhile, snap off and discard tough ends of asparagus; then cut stalks diagonally into 1-inch (2.5-cm) pieces.

4 Add asparagus to quinoa mixture and cook, stirring often, until asparagus is tender when pierced and almost all liquid has been absorbed (about 5 more minutes; reduce heat and stir more often as mixture thickens).

5 Remove pan from heat and gently stir in fontina cheese and chopped fresh sage (if using). Let stand until cheese is melted (about 2 minutes). Transfer to a shallow serving bowl or 4 individual bowls; top with Parmesan cheese and garnish with sage sprigs. Makes 4 servings.

Per serving: *356 calories (23% calories from fat), 9 g total fat, 4 g saturated fat, 17 mg cholesterol, 495 mg sodium, 54 g carbohydrates, 10 g fiber, 17g protein, 242 mg calcium, 6 mg iron*

Quinoa & Spinach Salad

½   cup (85 g) quinoa
1   cinnamon stick (about
     3 inches/8 cm long)
½   teaspoon cumin seeds
½   cup (120 ml) *each* unsweetened
     apple juice and water
3   tablespoons dried currants
2   cans (about 15 oz./425 g *each*)
     cannellini (white kidney
     beans), drained and rinsed
8   cups (about 8 oz./230 g)
     bite-size pieces rinsed, crisped
     fresh spinach
1   large red-skinned apple (about
     8 oz./230 g), cored and thinly
     sliced
⅓   cup (80 ml) cider vinegar
3   tablespoons (45 ml) honey
2   tablespoons (30 ml) salad oil

For a red, white, and green entrée, try this salad. It's based on toasted quinoa and fresh spinach; white beans and crisp red apple lend earthy-tasting and sweet accents.

Preparation time: 20 minutes   **Cooking time:** About 30 minutes

1 Place quinoa in a fine strainer and rinse thoroughly with cool water; drain well. Then place quinoa in a 1½- to 2-quart (1.4- to 1.9-liter) pan and cook over medium heat, stirring often, until darker in color (about 8 minutes). Add cinnamon stick, cumin seeds, apple juice, and water. Increase heat to medium-high and bring mixture to a boil; then reduce heat, cover, and simmer until almost all liquid has been absorbed and quinoa is tender to bite (about 15 minutes). Discard cinnamon stick; stir in currants and half the beans. Use quinoa mixture warm or cool.

2 In a large serving bowl, combine spinach, remaining beans, and apple. Mound quinoa mixture atop spinach mixture. In a small bowl, beat vinegar, honey, and oil until blended; pour over salad and mix gently but thoroughly. Makes 4 servings.

Per serving: *422 calories (20% calories from fat), 10 g total fat, 1 g saturated fat, 0 mg cholesterol, 336 mg sodium, 72 g carbohydrates, 15 g fiber, 16 g protein, 149 mg calcium, 7 mg iron*

Mushroom Bread Pudding with Wilted Spinach
(recipe on facing page)

Mushroom Bread Pudding with Wilted Spinach *(Pictured on facing page)*

Mushroom Bread Pudding:

1   package (about 1 oz./30 g) dried porcini

4   ounces (115 g) small button mushrooms

1   teaspoon butter or margarine

4   cloves garlic, minced or pressed

1½ teaspoons chopped fresh thyme or ¾ teaspoon dried thyme

1   large onion, chopped

2   large eggs

2   large egg whites

1   tablespoon cornstarch

1½ cups (360 ml) buttermilk

1¼ cups (300 ml) nonfat milk

2   teaspoons sugar

¼   teaspoon salt

⅛   teaspoon ground white pepper

8   slices whole wheat sandwich bread or egg sandwich bread (crusts removed), cut into 1-inch (2.5-cm) squares

Wilted Spinach:

1   pound (455 g) fresh spinach

1   tablespoon butter or margarine

⅛   teaspoon ground nutmeg (or to taste)

Salt and black pepper

Garnish:

Thyme sprigs (optional)

Mention bread pudding, and most people think of an old-fashioned dessert. But this pudding is a savory main course: squares of whole-grain bread baked in an herbed custard that's flavored with dried porcini and fresh button mushrooms. Serve the dish atop a bed of sautéed spinach.

Preparation time: 20 minutes   **Cooking time:** About 1¾ hours

1 Place porcini in a small bowl and add ½ cup (120 ml) boiling water. Let stand, stirring occasionally, until porcini are soft (about 10 minutes). Lift out porcini and, holding them over bowl, squeeze very dry; then coarsely chop and set aside. Without disturbing sediment at bottom of bowl, pour soaking liquid into a measuring cup; you should have about ¼ cup (60 ml). Set liquid aside; discard sediment.

2 While porcini are soaking, slice button mushrooms ¼ to ½ inch (6 mm to 1 cm) thick; set aside. Melt the 1 teaspoon butter in a wide nonstick frying pan over medium-high heat. Add garlic and chopped thyme; cook, stirring, until fragrant (about 30 seconds; do not scorch). Add button mushrooms, onion, and ¼ cup (60 ml) water; cook, stirring, until mushrooms are soft and browned bits stick to pan bottom (6 to 8 minutes). Add 2 tablespoons (30 ml) more water and remove pan from heat; stir to loosen any browned bits from pan. Transfer onion mixture to a small bowl and set aside.

3 In a large bowl, beat eggs and egg whites until well blended. Smoothly blend cornstarch with porcini soaking liquid; add cornstarch mixture, buttermilk, milk, sugar, the ¼ teaspoon salt, and white pepper to eggs and whisk until blended. Stir in onion mixture and chopped porcini. Add bread and mix gently but thoroughly; let stand until softened (about 5 minutes), stirring occasionally.

4 Transfer mixture to an 8-inch-square (20-cm-square) nonstick or greased regular baking pan. Set pan of pudding in a larger baking pan; then set on center rack of a 325°F (165°C) oven. Pour boiling water into larger pan up to level of pudding. Bake until top of pudding is golden brown and center no longer jiggles when pan is gently shaken (about 1 hour and 35 minutes).

5 When pudding is almost done, discard stems and any yellow or wilted leaves from spinach; rinse remaining leaves. Place half the spinach in a 4- to 5-quart (3.8- to 5-liter) pan. Cook over medium-high heat, stirring often, until wilted (2 to 4 minutes). Pour into a colander and drain well, then transfer to a bowl; keep warm. Repeat to cook remaining spinach. To cooked spinach, add the 1 tablespoon butter and nutmeg; season to taste with salt and black pepper and mix gently.

6 Divide spinach among 4 individual rimmed plates. Spoon pudding over spinach (or cut pudding into wedges and place atop spinach). Garnish with thyme sprigs, if desired. Makes 4 servings.

Per serving: *385 calories (25% calories from fat), 11 g total fat, 5 g saturated fat, 148 mg cholesterol, 716 mg sodium, 53 g carbohydrates, 4 g fiber, 21 g protein, 405 mg calcium, 7 mg iron*

Indonesian Brown Rice Salad

Brown Rice Salad:

2 cups (370 g) long-grain brown rice

2 cups (170 g) Chinese pea pods

1 medium-size red bell pepper

5 green onions

1 can (about 8 oz./230 g) water chestnuts, drained

¼ cup (10 g) cilantro leaves

1 cup (145 g) raisins

1 cup (144 g) roasted peanuts

Cilantro Sauce:

2 cups (470 ml) plain nonfat yogurt

½ cup (20 g) cilantro leaves

1 teaspoon Oriental sesame oil

½ teaspoon finely chopped garlic

¼ teaspoon salt (or to taste)

Lime Dressing:

⅔ cup (160 ml) unseasoned rice vinegar or cider vinegar

2 tablespoons (30 ml) *each* lime juice and reduced-sodium soy sauce

1 tablespoon minced fresh ginger

2 teaspoons finely chopped garlic

1 teaspoon honey

For a satisfying high-fiber salad, combine brown rice with crisp pea pods, water chestnuts and crunchy peanuts; then mix in a gingery soy-lime dresssing.

Preparation time: 25 minutes   **Cooking time:** About 45 minutes

1 In a 2½- to 3-quart (2.4- to 2.8-liter) pan, bring 4½ cups (1 liter) water to a boil over medium-high heat. Stir in rice; then reduce heat, cover, and simmer until liquid has been absorbed and rice is tender to bite (about 45 minutes). Transfer to a large bowl and let cool, stirring occasionally.

2 Meanwhile, remove and discard ends and strings of pea pods; thinly slice pea pods. Seed and chop bell pepper. Thinly slice onions; chop water chestnuts.

3 To cooled rice, add pea pods, bell pepper, onions, water chestnuts, the ¼ cup cilantro, raisins, and peanuts. Mix gently but thoroughly; set aside.

4 In a small serving bowl, combine yogurt, the ½ cup cilantro, oil, the ½ teaspoon garlic, and salt. Stir until blended; set aside.

5 In another small bowl, combine vinegar, lime juice, soy sauce, ginger, the 2 teaspoons garlic, and honey. Beat until blended; pour over salad and mix gently but thoroughly. Serve salad with cilantro sauce. Makes 8 servings.

Per serving: 545 calories (24% calories from fat), 15 g total fat, 2 g saturated fat, 2 mg cholesterol, 560 mg sodium, 90 g carbohydrates, 8 g fiber, 18 g protein, 218 mg calcium, 3 mg iron

Pepper, Rice & Cheese Casserole

1⅓ cups (247 g) long-grain white rice

4 large red or green bell peppers (about 2 lbs./905 g *total*)

1 large onion, chopped

2 cloves garlic, minced or pressed

1 cup (240 ml) vegetable broth

4 large eggs

About 2 cups (about 15 oz./425 g) part-skim ricotta cheese

¾ cup (60 g) grated Parmesan cheese

A creamy cheese topping covers rice dotted with onion and brilliant bell peppers in this colorful casserole.

Preparation time: 15 minutes   **Cooking time:** About 1½ hours

1 In a 3½- to 4-quart (3.3- to 3.8-liter) pan, bring 3 cups (710 ml) water to a boil over high heat. Stir in rice; then reduce heat, cover, and simmer until liquid has been absorbed and rice is tender to bite (about 20 minutes).

2 Meanwhile, seed bell peppers; then slice or chop them. Place peppers in a 5- to 6-quart (5- to 6-liter) pan and add onion, garlic, and ¼ cup (60 ml) of the broth. Cook over medium-high heat, stirring often, until liquid evaporates and browned bits stick to pan bottom (about 10 minutes). To deglaze pan, add water, 1 tablespoon (15 ml) at a time, if pan appears dry. Add ¼ cup (60 ml) more broth, stirring to loosen browned bits from pan. Remove pan from heat.

3 Stir cooked rice into pepper mixture; then spread mixture in a deep 3-quart (2.8-liter) casserole.

4 In a bowl, combine remaining ½ cup (120 ml) broth, eggs, ricotta cheese, and half the Parmesan cheese; beat until blended. Spread cheese mixture over rice mixture; sprinkle with remaining Parmesan cheese. Bake in a 375°F (190°C) oven until topping is golden brown (about 45 minutes). Makes 6 servings.

Per serving: 437 calories (28% calories from fat), 14 g total fat, 7 g saturated fat, 175 mg cholesterol, 503 mg sodium, 55 g carbohydrates, 3 g fiber, 23 g protein, 413 mg calcium, 3 mg iron

Wheat Berry Satay Salad

2   large yellow or white onions, thinly sliced

2   cups (250 g) wheat berries, rinsed and drained

3   cups (710 ml) vegetable broth

    About ⅛ teaspoon crushed red pepper flakes (or to taste)

1   tablespoon finely chopped fresh ginger

2   tablespoons creamy peanut butter

2   tablespoons fruit or berry jam or jelly

2   tablespoons (30 ml) seasoned rice vinegar (or 2 table-spoons/30 ml distilled white vinegar plus ½ to 1 teaspoon sugar)

    About 1 tablespoon (15 ml) reduced-sodium soy sauce (or to taste)

1   cup (40 g) chopped cilantro

1   cup (100 g) sliced green onions

¼   cup (36 g) finely chopped salted roasted peanuts

Spiked with ginger and red pepper flakes, this salad of broth-simmered wheat berries (whole, unprocessed wheat kernels) is dressed with an Indonesian-style spicy peanut sauce. Wheat berries are sold, packaged or in bulk, in health food stores and many well-stocked supermarkets.

Preparation time: 15 minutes, plus about 30 minutes for salad to cool **Cooking time:** About 1¾ hours

1 In a 4- to 5-quart (3.8- to 5-liter) pan, combine yellow onions and ½ cup (120 ml) water. Cook over medium-high heat, stirring often, until liquid evaporates and browned bits stick to pan bottom (10 to 15 minutes). To deglaze pan, add ¼ cup (60 ml) more water, stirring to loosen browned bits from pan; continue to cook until browned bits form again. Repeat deglazing step 3 or 4 more times or until onions are dark brown, using ¼ cup (60 ml) water each time.

2 Add wheat berries, broth, red pepper flakes, and ginger to pan. Bring to a boil; then reduce heat, cover, and simmer, stirring occasionally, until wheat berries are just tender to bite (50 to 60 minutes). Remove from heat; drain and reserve cooking liquid.

3 In a small bowl, beat ¼ cup (60 ml) of the reserved cooking liquid, peanut butter, and jam until smoothly blended. Stir peanut butter mixture, vinegar, and soy sauce into wheat berry mixture. Cover salad and let stand until cool (about 30 minutes).

4 Add two-thirds each of the cilantro and green onions to salad; mix gently but thoroughly. If a moister texture is desired, mix in some of the remaining cooking liquid. Transfer salad to a serving bowl; sprinkle with remaining cilantro, remaining green onions, and peanuts. Makes 4 servings.

Per serving: *517 calories (19% calories from fat), 12 g total fat, 1 g saturated fat, 0 mg cholesterol, 1,136 mg sodium, 92 g carbohydrates, 18 g fiber, 19 g protein, 96 mg calcium, 4 mg iron*

Wheat Germ Burgers *(Pictured on facing page)*

2 large eggs

¾ cup (72 g) toasted wheat germ

½ cup (55 g) shredded reduced-fat jack cheese

¼ cup (20 g) chopped mushrooms

3 tablespoons finely chopped onion

½ teaspoon *each* dried thyme and dried rosemary, crumbled

1½ cups (150 g) long zucchini shreds

Salt and pepper

1 to 2 teaspoons salad oil

4 kaiser rolls or hamburger buns

½ cup (120 ml) plain nonfat yogurt

About ¼ cup (60 ml) catsup

About 2 tablespoons Dijon mustard

4 to 8 butter lettuce leaves, rinsed and crisped

1 large tomato (about 8 oz./ 230 g), thinly sliced

Toasted wheat germ, shredded zucchini, and fresh herbs come together in these winning meatless burgers. Serve them with low-fat embellishments, such as catsup, Dijon mustard, and spoonfuls of plain yogurt.

Preparation time: 20 minutes　　**Cooking time:** About 10 minutes

1 In a large bowl, beat eggs to blend. Stir in wheat germ, cheese, mushrooms, onion, thyme, rosemary, and zucchini. Season to taste with salt and pepper.

2 On plastic wrap, shape wheat germ mixture into 4 equal patties, each about ¾ inch (2 cm) thick.

3 Heat 1 teaspoon of the oil in a wide nonstick frying pan over medium heat. Add patties and cook until deep golden on bottom (4 to 5 minutes). Turn patties over; add 1 teaspoon more oil to pan, if needed. Cook until deep golden on other side (about 4 more minutes).

4 To serve, place patties on bottoms of buns. Top with yogurt, catsup, mustard, lettuce leaves, and tomato, then with tops of buns. Makes 4 servings.

Per serving: *416 calories (27% calories from fat), 13 g total fat, 4 g saturated fat, 117 mg cholesterol, 885 mg sodium, 54 g carbohydrates, 5 g fiber, 22 g protein, 311 mg calcium, 5 mg iron*

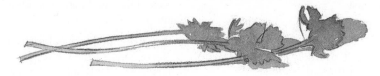

Double Wheat Burgers

2 large eggs

1 cup (45 g) soft whole wheat bread crumbs

½ cup (48 g) toasted wheat germ

¼ cup (30 g) chopped walnuts

½ cup (50 g) sliced green onions

½ cup (120 ml) small-curd low-fat (1%) cottage cheese

2 tablespoons chopped parsley

1 teaspoon dried basil

½ teaspoon *each* dried oregano and paprika

Salt

4 thin slices reduced-fat jack cheese (about 2 oz./55 g *total*)

4 whole wheat hamburger buns, toasted

¼ cup (60 ml) nonfat Thousand Island dressing or mayonnaise

1 very large tomato (about 10 oz./285 g), thinly sliced

1 small white onion, thinly sliced

4 to 8 red leaf lettuce leaves, rinsed and crisped

Herbed wheat germ and walnut patties served on whole wheat buns make a filling lunch or dinner. Dress up the burgers with lettuce, slices of tomato and onion, and creamy Thousand Island dressing.

Preparation time: 15 minutes　　**Cooking time:** About 7 minutes

1 In a large bowl, beat eggs to blend. Stir in bread crumbs, wheat germ, walnuts, green onions, cottage cheese, parsley, basil, oregano, and paprika. Season to taste with salt.

2 On an oiled 12- by 15-inch (30- by 38-cm) baking sheet, shape mixture into 4 equal patties, each about ½ inch (1 cm) thick. Broil patties about 3 inches (8 cm) below heat, turning once, until deep golden on both sides (about 6 minutes). Top each patty with a slice of jack cheese and continue to broil just until cheese is melted (about 30 more seconds).

3 To serve, place patties on bottoms of buns. Top with dressing, tomato, onion slices, and lettuce, then with tops of buns. Makes 4 servings.

Per serving: *424 calories (30% calories from fat), 15 g total fat, 4 g saturated fat, 117 mg cholesterol, 784 mg sodium, 54 g carbohydrates, 9 g fiber, 24 g protein, 259 mg calcium, 5 mg iron*

Wheat Germ Burgers
(recipe on facing page)

Almost Vegetarian Whole Grains

✳

Oat Pilaf with Beef, Hazelnuts & Scotch

Preparation time: *25 minutes*
Cooking time: *About 1 hour*

12	ounces (340 g) lean boneless top sirloin steak (about 1 inch/2.5 cm thick), trimmed of fat and cut across the grain into ⅛- by 2-inch (3-mm by 5-cm) strips
1	tablespoon (15 ml) reduced-sodium soy sauce
1	teaspoon sugar
½	teaspoon lemon juice
1	clove garlic, minced or pressed
⅓	cup (50 g) hazelnuts
1	large onion, chopped
6	cups (1.4 liters) vegetable broth
3	cups (510 g) oat groats (uncut oats)
1	teaspoon salad oil
	About 6 tablespoons (90 ml) Scotch whiskey (or to taste)
½	cup (50 g) thinly sliced green onions

In a large bowl, combine beef, soy sauce, sugar, lemon juice, and garlic. Set aside; stir occasionally.

Spread hazelnuts in a shallow 3- to 3½-quart (2.8- to 3.3-liter) casserole, about 9 by 13 inches (23 by 33 cm). Bake in a 350°F (175°C) oven, shaking casserole occasionally, until nuts are lightly browned under skins (10 to 15 minutes). Pour nuts onto a towel; rub with towel to remove as much of the skins as possible. Lift nuts from towel; discard skins. Coarsely chop nuts and set aside.

In a 3- to 4-quart (2.8- to 3.8-liter) pan, combine chopped onion and ¼ cup (60 ml) water. Cook over medium-high heat, stirring often, until onion is soft (about 5 minutes); add water, 1 tablespoon (15 ml) at a time, if pan appears dry. Transfer onion to casserole used to toast nuts; set aside.

In pan used to cook onion, combine broth and oats. Bring just to a boil over medium-high heat. Add broth-oat mixture to casserole. Cover tightly and bake in a 350°F (175°C) oven for 15 minutes. Stir well, cover tightly again, and continue to bake until almost all liquid has been absorbed and oats are tender to bite (about 15 more minutes).

Meanwhile, heat oil in a wide non-stick frying pan over medium-high heat. Lift meat from marinade and drain briefly; discard marinade. Add meat to pan and cook, stirring often, until done to your liking; cut to test (2 to 3 minutes for rare). With a slotted spoon, transfer meat to a bowl and keep warm; discard pan drippings.

Uncover oat pilaf and stir in 6 tablespoons of the Scotch. Spoon pilaf onto a rimmed platter and top with meat (and any juices that have accumulated in bowl). Sprinkle with green onions and hazelnuts. Offer additional Scotch to add to taste. Makes 6 servings.

Per serving: 526 calories (29% calories from fat), 16 g total fat, 3 g saturated fat, 42 mg cholesterol, 1,084 mg sodium, 60 g carbohydrates, 1 g fiber, 28 g protein, 73 mg calcium, 6 mg iron

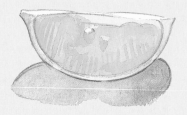

Mahogany Rice, Sausage & Fennel in Squash Bowls

Preparation time: *20 minutes*
Cooking time: *About 1 hour and 20 minutes*

2	medium-size acorn squash (about 3½ lbs./1.6 kg *total*)
1	head fennel (3 to 4 inches/8 to 10 cm in diameter, about 1 lb./455 g)
8	ounces (230 g) mild turkey Italian sausage, casings removed
2	tablespoons (30 ml) balsamic vinegar
4½	cups (1.1 liters) vegetable broth
1	cup (185 g) red or black (Wehani or Black Japonica) rice (sold in natural food stores), rinsed and drained

Cut squash in half lengthwise; scoop out and discard seeds and fibers. Place squash halves, cut side down, in a 9- by 13-inch (23- by 33-cm) baking pan. Pour water into pan to a depth of about ½ inch (1 cm); bake in a 400°F (205°C) oven until squash is tender when pierced (about 50 minutes). Drain liquid from pan and keep squash warm.

Meanwhile, trim stems from fennel; reserve feathery green leaves, then discard stems. Trim and discard discolored parts of fennel. Thinly slice fennel, place in a 5- to 6-quart (5- to 6-liter) pan, and add sausage. Cook over medium-high heat, stirring often, until mixture is well browned (about 15 minutes). Then spoon off and discard any fat from pan.

Add vinegar and ½ cup (120 ml) of the broth to pan. Cook, stirring often, until liquid evaporates and browned bits stick to pan bottom (about 10 minutes). To deglaze pan, add ½ cup (120 ml) more broth, stirring to loosen browned bits from pan; continue to cook until browned bits form again. Add rice and remaining 3½ cups (830 ml) broth, stirring to loosen browned bits. Bring to a boil; then reduce heat, cover, and simmer until rice is tender to bite (about 50 minutes).

Meanwhile, finely chop about half the reserved fennel leaves. When rice is done, remove from heat and stir in chopped fennel leaves. Place squash halves, cut side up, on a platter or individual plates. Fill squash with rice mixture; sprinkle with remaining fennel leaves. Makes 4 servings.

Per serving: 405 calories (19% calories from fat), 9 g total fat, 2 g saturated fat, 43 mg cholesterol, 1,559 mg sodium, 69 g carbohydrates, 11 g fiber, 17 g protein, 133 mg calcium, 3 mg iron

Creamy Barley with Chicken

Preparation time: *15 minutes*
Cooking time: *About 40 minutes*

2 teaspoons olive oil
2 boneless, skinless chicken breast halves (about 12 oz./340 g *total*), cut into ¾-inch (2-cm) pieces
⅛ teaspoon salt (or to taste)
1 large onion, chopped
1½ teaspoons chopped fresh sage or ¾ teaspoon dried rubbed sage
¼ teaspoon pepper
3½ cups (830 ml) vegetable broth
1⅓ cups (270 g) pearl barley, rinsed and drained
1 package (about 10 oz./285 g) frozen corn kernels, thawed and drained

1 can (about 15 oz./425 g) cream-style corn
¼ cup (15 g) finely chopped parsley
Sage sprigs (optional)

Heat oil in a 4- to 5-quart (3.8- to 5-liter) pan over medium-high heat. Add chicken and salt. Cook, stirring often, until chicken is no longer pink in center; cut to test (2 to 3 minutes). Remove from pan with a slotted spoon and set aside. Add onion, chopped sage, pepper, and ¼ cup (60 ml) water to pan. Cook, stirring often, until onion is soft (about 5 minutes).

Stir in broth and barley and bring to a boil; then reduce heat, cover, and simmer until barley is tender to bite (about 30 minutes). Add corn kernels, cream-style corn, and chicken. Cook, stirring, just until heated through. Spoon barley mixture onto a rimmed platter and sprinkle with parsley. Garnish with sage sprigs, if desired. Makes 6 servings.

Per serving: 352 calories (10% calories from fat), 4 g total fat, 1 g saturated fat, 33 mg cholesterol, 874 mg sodium, 62 g carbohydrates, 9 g fiber, 21 g protein, 36 mg calcium, 2 mg iron

Oven-baked Paella

Preparation time: *25 minutes*
Cooking time: *About 1 hour and 5 minutes*

2 cups (370 g) long-grain brown rice
6 ounces (170 g) reduced-fat mild or hot Italian sausage, casings removed
4 cups (950 ml) vegetable broth
2 cloves garlic, minced or pressed
⅛ teaspoon ground saffron or a large pinch of saffron threads (or to taste)

1 can (about 15 oz./425 g) cannellini (white kidney beans), drained and rinsed
1 package (about 10 oz./285 g) frozen tiny peas, thawed and drained
1 large tomato (about 8 oz./230 g), coarsely chopped and drained
½ cup (50 g) thinly sliced green onions
8 ounces (230 g) small cooked shrimp
Lemon wedges

Spread rice in a shallow 3- to 3½-quart (2.8- to 3.3-liter) casserole, about 9 by 13 inches (23 by 33 cm). Bake in a 350°F (175°C) oven, stirring occasionally, until rice is golden brown (about 25 minutes).

Meanwhile, coarsely chop or crumble sausage; then place in a 3- to 4-quart (2.8- to 3.8-liter) pan and cook over medium-high heat, stirring often, until no longer pink (5 to 7 minutes). Remove sausage from pan and set aside; pour off and discard any fat from pan.

In same pan, combine 3½ cups (830 ml) of the broth, 2½ cups (590 ml) water, garlic, and saffron. Bring just to a boil over medium-high heat. Leaving casserole on oven rack, carefully stir broth mixture and sausage into rice. Cover tightly and bake until almost all liquid has been absorbed (about 40 minutes); stir after 20 and 30 minutes, covering casserole tightly again each time.

Uncover casserole; stir in remaining ½ cup (120 ml) broth, beans, peas, and tomato. Bake, uncovered, for 5 more minutes. Remove casserole from oven; stir in onions, then sprinkle with shrimp. Garnish with lemon wedges. Makes 8 servings.

Per serving: 322 calories (15% calories from fat), 5 g total fat, 1 g saturated fat, 61 mg cholesterol, 905 mg sodium, 51 g carbohydrates, 3 g fiber, 18 g protein, 49 mg calcium, 3 mg iron

Kidney Cobb Salad
(recipe on page 56)

LEGUMES

*S*atisfying is the word for these entrées. Some are served hot, others cool, but all are just right for hearty appetites and hungry diners. If you're looking for meatless versions of traditional favorites, bake a golden-crusted pot pie filled with chili-seasoned beans and tiny onions, or present a rich, spicy curry based on nutty garbanzos. If you're in the mood for more unusual recipes, you'll find those too: try a creamy white bean stew tinted and flavored with saffron and juicy fresh apricots, or a maple-sauced combination of mild tofu and apples served in baked acorn squash "bowls."

Kidney Cobb Salad *(Pictured on page 54)*

Dressing:

⅓ cup (80 ml) *each* nonfat mayon-
    naise and nonfat sour cream

2   tablespoons (30 ml) *each*
    balsamic vinegar and smooth
    unsweetened applesauce

1   tablespoon (15 ml) *each* olive
    oil and Dijon mustard

1   tablespoon chopped fresh dill
    or 1 teaspoon dried dill weed

1   teaspoon sugar (or to taste)
    Dill sprigs (optional)

Salad:

2   cans (about 15 oz./425 g *each*)
    red kidney beans

1   large yellow or red bell pepper
    (about 8 oz./230 g)

6   ounces (170 g) feta cheese

1   very small red onion (about 4
    oz./115 g)

1   large head red leaf lettuce
    (1½ lbs./680 g), separated into
    leaves, rinsed, and crisped

1   package (about 10 oz./285 g)
    frozen tiny peas, thawed and
    drained

This hearty main dish resembles the classic Cobb Salad in that the ingredients are arranged spoke-fashion on the serving platter—but that's where the similarity ends. We've replaced the traditional chicken, bacon, avocado, and blue cheese with beans, green peas, golden bell pepper, and tangy feta. Serve with chilled mineral water or iced tea, if you like.

Preparation time: 20 minutes

1 In a small bowl, combine mayonnaise, sour cream, vinegar, applesauce, oil, mustard, chopped dill, and sugar. Beat until smoothly blended. If a thinner dressing is desired, add water, 1 tablespoon (15 ml) at a time, until dressing has the desired consistency. Spoon into a small serving bowl; garnish with dill sprigs, if desired. Cover lightly and refrigerate while you prepare salad.

2 Drain beans and rinse well. Seed and finely chop bell pepper. Crumble cheese. Thinly slice onion; separate slices into rings.

3 To assemble salad, line a rimmed platter or a wide salad bowl with large lettuce leaves, then break remaining leaves into bite-size pieces and arrange atop whole leaves. Mound peas, beans, bell pepper, and cheese separately on lettuce; place onion in center. Offer dressing to add to taste. Makes 6 servings.

Per serving: *256 calories (26% calories from fat), 7 g total fat, 4 g saturated fat, 25 mg cholesterol, 718 mg sodium, 32 g carbohydrates, 9 g fiber, 16 g protein, 279 mg calcium, 4 mg iron*

Black Bean Chili with Oranges

2   large onions, chopped

2   cloves garlic, minced or
    pressed

1   tablespoon (15 ml) salad oil

3   cans (about 15 oz./425 g *each*)
    black beans, drained and
    rinsed well

1   cup (240 ml) vegetable broth

1   tablespoon coriander seeds

1   teaspoon dried oregano

¼   teaspoon ground allspice
    About ⅛ teaspoon crushed red
    pepper flakes (or to taste)

⅛   teaspoon ground cardamom

4   large navel oranges (2 to 2½
    lbs./905 g to 1.15 kg *total*)

1   cup (240 ml) nonfat sour cream
    Salt

Looking for a warming dish for winter days? Serve aromatic black bean chili laced with orange juice and peel, then topped with refreshing orange slices.

Preparation time: 25 minutes   **Cooking time:** About 40 minutes

1 In a 5- to 6-quart (5- to 6-liter) pan, combine onions, garlic, oil, and ¼ cup (60 ml) water. Cook over medium-high heat, stirring often, until onions are tinged with brown (about 10 minutes); add water, 1 tablespoon (15 ml) at a time, if pan appears dry. Add beans, broth, coriander seeds, oregano, allspice, red pepper flakes, and cardamom. Bring to a boil; then reduce heat, cover, and simmer until flavors are blended (about 10 minutes).

2 Meanwhile, finely shred enough peel (colored part only) from oranges to make 2 teaspoons. Squeeze juice from enough oranges to make ½ cup (120 ml). Set shredded peel and juice aside. Cut peel and all white membrane from remaining oranges; thinly slice fruit crosswise. Cover sliced oranges and set aside.

3 Uncover chili; bring to a boil over medium heat. Then boil, stirring occasionally, until thickened (15 to 20 minutes; as chili thickens, reduce heat and stir more often). Stir 1 teaspoon of the orange peel and the ½ cup (120 ml) orange juice into chili. Ladle chili into bowls; top with orange slices and sour cream. Garnish with remaining 1 teaspoon orange peel. Season to taste with salt. Makes 4 servings.

Per serving: *383 calories (13% calories from fat), 6 g total fat, 0.6 g saturated fat, 0 mg cholesterol, 810 mg sodium, 66 g carbohydrates, 15 g fiber, 19 g protein, 251 mg calcium, 4 mg iron*

Southwestern Stuffed Peppers

2   very large red, yellow, or green bell peppers (about 10 oz./ 285 g *each*); choose wide, squarish peppers

¼   cup (30 g) slivered almonds

1   package (about 10 oz./285 g) frozen corn kernels, thawed and drained

1   can (about 15 oz./425 g) black beans, drained and rinsed well

1   can (about 8 oz./230 g) tomato sauce

½   cup (75 g) raisins or dried currants

½   cup (50 g) sliced green onions

2   teaspoons cider vinegar

2   cloves garlic, minced

½   teaspoon *each* ground cinnamon and chili powder

1/16   to ⅛ teaspoon ground cloves Salt

½   cup (55 g) shredded reduced-fat jack cheese

2   tablespoons cilantro leaves

1   cup (240 ml) plain nonfat yogurt

Vivid red bell peppers make bright edible containers for a sweet-spicy black bean and corn filling.

Preparation time: 30 minutes   **Cooking time:** About 45 minutes

1. Using a very sharp knife, carefully cut each pepper in half lengthwise through (and including) stem; leave stem attached and remove seeds. If any of the pepper halves does not sit flat, even out the base by trimming a thin slice from it (do not pierce wall of pepper). Set pepper halves aside.

2. Toast almonds in a 5- to 6-quart (5- to 6-liter) pan over medium heat, stirring often, until golden (about 3 minutes). Transfer almonds to a bowl and let cool; then coarsely chop and set aside.

3. In same pan, bring 3 to 4 quarts (2.8 to 3.8 liters) water to a boil over medium-high heat. Add pepper halves and cook for 2 minutes. Lift out, drain, and set aside. Discard water and dry pan. In pan (off heat) or in a large bowl, combine corn, beans, tomato sauce, raisins, onions, vinegar, garlic, cinnamon, chili powder, and cloves. Mix gently but thoroughly; season to taste with salt.

4. Spoon vegetable mixture equally into pepper halves, mounding filling at top. Set pepper halves, filled side up, in a 9- by 13-inch (23- by 33-cm) baking pan. Cover and bake in a 375°F (190°C) oven for 10 minutes. Uncover and continue to bake until filling is hot in center (about 20 more minutes; if drippings begin to scorch, carefully add about ¼ cup/60 ml water to pan). Remove from oven and sprinkle evenly with cheese; cover and let stand for 5 minutes. Garnish with cilantro; offer yogurt to add to taste. Makes 4 servings.

Per serving: *353 calories (20% calories from fat), 8 g total fat, 2 g saturated fat, 11 mg cholesterol, 678 mg sodium, 58 g carbohydrates, 9 g fiber, 18 g protein, 327 mg calcium, 3 mg iron*

Curried Garbanzo Beans

1   teaspoon olive oil

1   large onion, chopped

4   cloves garlic, minced

½   teaspoon ground coriander

¼   teaspoon ground ginger

⅛   teaspoon ground red pepper (cayenne), or to taste

¼   cup (10 g) cilantro leaves

2   large tomatoes (about 1 lb./ 455 g *total*), chopped

2   teaspoons butter or margarine

⅛   teaspoon ground turmeric

2   cans (about 15 oz./425 g *each*) garbanzo beans, drained and rinsed

½   cup (120 ml) vegetable broth

2   teaspoons lime juice Salt

1½   cups (360 ml) plain nonfat yogurt Lime wedges

This mild, distinctive curry goes together quickly. Fresh tomatoes enrich the aromatic sauce and garnish the finished dish.

Preparation time: 20 minutes   **Cooking time:** About 30 minutes

1. Heat oil in a 3- to 4-quart (2.8- to 3.8-liter) pan over medium-high heat. Add onion, garlic, coriander, ginger, red pepper, and ¼ cup (60 ml) water. Cook, stirring often, until onion is soft (about 5 minutes; do not scorch). Add water, 1 tablespoon (15 ml) at a time, if pan appears dry. Stir in cilantro and half the tomatoes. Cook, stirring often, just until tomatoes are soft (about 3 minutes).

2. Carefully transfer onion mixture to a food processor or blender. Whirl until smoothly puréed. Return to pan; add butter and turmeric. Bring just to a boil over medium-high heat (2 to 3 minutes). Add beans, broth, and lime juice. Return to a boil; then reduce heat, cover, and simmer for 15 minutes.

3. Spoon curry into wide individual bowls; sprinkle remaining tomatoes evenly around edge of each bowl. Season to taste with salt; offer yogurt and lime to add to taste. Makes 4 servings.

Per serving: *275 calories (23% calories from fat), 7 g total fat, 2 g saturated fat, 7 mg cholesterol, 457 mg sodium, 40 g carbohydrates, 8 g fiber, 14 g protein, 238 mg calcium, 3 mg iron*

Bean Roll-ups *(Pictured on facing page)*

1 package (about 10 oz./285 g) frozen chopped spinach, thawed and squeezed dry

1 large package (about 8 oz./230 g) nonfat cream cheese or Neufchâtel cheese, at room temperature

½ cup (40 g) grated Parmesan cheese

2 tablespoons (30 ml) nonfat mayonnaise

1 teaspoon prepared horseradish (or to taste)

1/16 teaspoon ground allspice (or to taste)

1 can (about 15 oz./425 g) cannellini (white kidney beans)

1 tablespoon (15 ml) seasoned rice vinegar (or 1 tablespoon/15 ml distilled white vinegar plus ½ teaspoon sugar)

2 teaspoons honey

¾ teaspoon chopped fresh thyme or ¼ teaspoon dried thyme

⅓ cup (35 g) thinly sliced green onions

⅓ cup (20 g) finely chopped parsley

6 reduced-fat flour tortillas (*each about 7 inches/18 cm in diameter*)

About 48 whole fresh spinach leaves, rinsed and crisped

Thyme sprigs (optional)

A spinach-flecked cheese spread and a zesty bean filling are wrapped inside flour tortillas to make these cool sandwiches. Try them for lunch on a warm summer day, perhaps with a fresh fruit salad alongside.

Preparation time: 25 minutes

1 In a medium-size bowl, combine chopped spinach, cream cheese, Parmesan cheese, mayonnaise, horseradish, and allspice. Mix well; set aside.

2 Drain beans, reserving liquid. Rinse beans well, place in another medium-size bowl, and add vinegar, honey, and chopped thyme. Coarsely mash beans with a spoon; add enough of the reserved bean liquid to give mixture a spreadable consistency (do not make it too thin). Set aside. In a small bowl, combine onions and parsley; set aside.

3 To assemble sandwiches, divide spinach mixture equally among tortillas. With a spatula, spread spinach mixture to cover tortillas evenly. Then top tortillas equally with bean filling; carefully spread to cover spinach mixture. Sprinkle with onion mixture. Roll up each tortilla tightly to enclose filling. (At this point, you may cover tightly and refrigerate for up to 3 hours.)

4 Line 6 individual plates with spinach leaves. With a serrated knife, carefully cut each tortilla diagonally into 4 equal slices (wipe knife clean between cuts, if desired); arrange on spinach-lined plates. Garnish with thyme sprigs, if desired. Makes 6 servings.

Per serving: 230 calories (17% calories from fat), 4 g total fat, 1 g saturated fat, 9 mg cholesterol, 964 mg sodium, 33 g carbohydrates, 7 g fiber, 15 g protein, 388 mg calcium, 3 mg iron

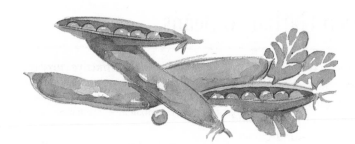

Bean Roll-ups
(recipe on facing page)

Garbanzo Antipasto Salad

8   ounces (230 g) sourdough bread, cut into about ½-inch (1-cm) cubes

½   cup (120 ml) white wine vinegar

2   tablespoons (30 ml) olive oil

1   tablespoon chopped fresh oregano or 1 teaspoon dried oregano

2   teaspoons honey (or to taste)

2   cloves garlic, minced or pressed

⅛   to ¼ teaspoon pepper

2   cans (about 15 oz./425 g *each*) garbanzo beans, drained and rinsed

2   large tomatoes (about 1 lb./ 455 g *total*), chopped and drained well

¼   cup (25 g) slivered red onion, in about 1-inch (2.5-cm) lengths

¼   cup (45 g) oil-cured olives, pitted and sliced

3   to 4 tablespoons drained capers

⅓   cup (80 ml) *each* nonfat mayonnaise and nonfat sour cream

2   tablespoons chopped fresh dill or 2 teaspoons dried dill weed

8   to 12 butter lettuce leaves, rinsed and crisped

Garbanzo beans, ripe tomatoes, and crisp homemade croutons team up with tart capers and olives in this zesty marinated salad. A cool, creamy dill dressing adds the finishing touch.

Preparation time: 30 minutes, plus at least 1 hour to chill   **Cooking time:** 15 to 20 minutes

1 Spread bread cubes in a single layer in a shallow 10- by 15-inch (25- by 38-cm) baking pan. Bake in a 325°F (165°C) oven, stirring occasionally, until crisp and tinged with brown (15 to 20 minutes). Set aside. If made ahead, let cool completely in pan on a rack, then store airtight for up to 2 days.

2 In a large bowl, combine vinegar, oil, oregano, honey, garlic, and pepper. Beat until blended. Add beans, tomatoes, onion, olives, and capers; mix gently but thoroughly. Cover and refrigerate for at least 1 hour or up to 4 hours.

3 Meanwhile, in a small bowl, beat mayonnaise, sour cream, and dill until smoothly blended; cover and refrigerate.

4 To serve, line 4 individual rimmed plates or shallow bowls with lettuce leaves. Add croutons to salad and mix gently but thoroughly, being sure to coat croutons with marinade. Then, using a slotted spoon, transfer salad to plates; top each serving with a dollop of dill dressing. Makes 4 servings.

Per serving: *466 calories (30% calories from fat), 15 g total fat, 2 g saturated fat, 0 mg cholesterol, 1,234 mg sodium, 67 g carbohydrates, 9 g fiber, 16 g protein, 144 mg calcium, 5 mg iron*

Peanut Stew with Banana Couscous

1   can (about 12 oz./360 ml)
     banana nectar
     About 1¼ cups (300 ml)
     low-fat (2%) milk

1   medium-size red onion (about
     8 oz./230 g), finely chopped

1   can (about 20 oz./570 g)
     crushed pineapple packed in
     its own juice

1   medium-size very ripe banana
     (about 6 oz./170 g), mashed

1   package (about 10 oz./285 g)
     frozen chopped spinach,
     thawed and squeezed dry

½   cup (120 ml) crunchy peanut
     butter
     About ⅛ teaspoon crushed red
     pepper flakes

1   package (about 10 oz./285 g)
     couscous

¼   cup (10 g) *each* coarsely chopped
     fresh mint and cilantro
     Lime wedges

Pineapple, ripe banana, and a hearty helping of peanut butter give this fruit-and-vegetable stew its rich, slightly sweet flavor. Serve the dish over creamy couscous simmered in a fragrant blend of milk and banana nectar.

Preparation time: 20 minutes   **Cooking time:** About 20 minutes

1   Pour banana nectar into a 4-cup (950-ml) glass measure. Add enough milk to make 2¾ cups (650 ml); set aside.

2   In a wide nonstick frying pan, combine onion and ¼ cup (60 ml) water. Cook over medium-high heat, stirring often, until onion is soft (about 5 minutes); add water, 1 tablespoon (15 ml) at a time, if pan appears dry.

3   Add undrained pineapple and mashed banana to onion mixture; bring to a boil. Stir in spinach; then reduce heat, cover, and simmer for 5 minutes. Add peanut butter and red pepper flakes. Simmer, uncovered, for 5 minutes, stirring until peanut butter is melted and smoothly blended into sauce.

4   Meanwhile, pour milk mixture into a 2- to 3-quart (1.9- to 2.8-liter) pan and bring just to a boil over medium-high heat. Stir in couscous. Cover, remove from heat, and let stand until liquid has been absorbed (5 to 6 minutes).

5   Spoon couscous into 4 wide individual bowls and top with spinach mixture. Sprinkle with mint and cilantro; garnish with lime wedges. Makes 4 servings.

Per serving: *696 calories (23% calories from fat), 19 g total fat, 4 g saturated fat, 6 mg cholesterol, 271 mg sodium, 115 g carbohydrates, 8 g fiber, 23 g protein, 243 mg calcium, 4 mg iron*

Mediterranean Nachos with Pita Chips

4   whole wheat pita breads (*each*
     about 5 inches/12.5 cm in
     diameter), cut crosswise into
     halves

1   pound (455 g) carrots (about 8
     small carrots), cut into 1-inch
     (2.5-cm) lengths

2   cans (about 15 oz./425 g *each*)
     garbanzo beans, drained and
     rinsed

¼   cup (60 ml) lemon juice

3   or 4 cloves garlic, peeled

4   teaspoons (20 ml) Oriental
     sesame oil
     Salt

1   jar (about 7 oz./200 g) roasted
     red peppers, drained, rinsed,
     and coarsely chopped

1   cup (about 4 oz./115 g) shred-
     ded reduced-fat jack cheese
     Lemon wedges

1   cup (240 ml) plain nonfat
     yogurt

Golden, garlicky hummus sweetened with carrots makes an unusual and colorful topping for nachos. And here's another twist: in place of the typical tortilla chips, we use crisp triangles made from whole wheat pita bread.

Preparation time: 20 minutes   **Cooking time:** About 25 minutes

1   Carefully peel pita bread halves apart; stack halves, then cut stack into 3 equal wedges. Spread wedges in a single layer on 2 large baking sheets. Bake in a 350°F (175°C) oven until browned and crisp (about 15 minutes), switching positions of baking sheets halfway through baking. Let cool on baking sheets on racks.

2   Meanwhile, in a 2- to 3-quart (1.9- to 2.8-liter) pan, combine carrots and 4 cups (950 ml) water. Bring to a boil over medium-high heat; then reduce heat, cover, and simmer, stirring occasionally, until carrots are tender when pierced but still bright in color (about 15 minutes). Drain well.

3   Pour carrots into a food processor or blender and add beans, lemon juice, garlic, and oil. Whirl until smoothly puréed, scraping sides of container often. Season to taste with salt. Spoon bean mixture onto a large ovenproof rimmed platter; spread out to make an oval. Top with red peppers and sprinkle with cheese.

4   Bake in a 400°F (205°C) oven until bean mixture is hot in center (about 10 minutes). Remove from oven. Tuck some of the pita chips around edge of platter; serve remaining chips alongside. Garnish with lemon wedges. Offer yogurt to spoon over nachos to taste. Makes 4 servings.

Per serving: *535 calories (24% calories from fat), 15 g total fat, 5 g saturated fat, 21 mg cholesterol, 982 mg sodium, 76 g carbohydrates, 14 g fiber, 27 g protein, 448 mg calcium, 4 mg iron*

Chili Pot Pie
(recipe on facing page)

Chili Pot Pie *(Pictured on facing page)*

Chili:

1 tablespoon chili powder (or to taste)

2 tablespoons pure maple syrup

1½ teaspoons dry mustard

1½ teaspoons Worcestershire or reduced-sodium soy sauce

2 cloves garlic, minced or pressed

1 can (about 15 oz./425 g) pinto beans, drained and rinsed

1 package (about 1 lb./455 g) frozen mixed bell pepper strips, thawed and drained; or about 4 cups fresh yellow, red, and green bell pepper strips (or use all of one color)

1 package (about 10 oz./285 g) frozen tiny onions, thawed and drained

1 large tomato (about 8 oz./ 230 g), chopped

¼ cup (35 g) yellow cornmeal

Pastry:

⅔ cup (160 ml) low-fat (2%) cottage cheese

⅓ cup (76 g) butter or margarine, cut into chunks

1 large egg

¼ cup (60 ml) smooth unsweetened applesauce

¼ teaspoon *each* ground cumin and salt

1⅔ cups (210 g) bread flour or all-purpose flour

2 tablespoons (30 ml) nonfat milk

This savory pot pie is filled with a colorful chili made from pinto beans, bell pepper strips, and tiny sweet onions. You might serve it with a crisp green salad and a platter of juicy orange wedges. We call for Worcestershire as a seasoning, but since it's made with anchovies (or other fish), strict vegetarians will want to use soy sauce instead.

Preparation time: 30 minutes　　**Cooking time:** About 1 hour

1　In a large bowl, combine chili powder, syrup, mustard, Worcestershire, and garlic. Add beans, bell peppers, onions, and tomato. Mix gently but thoroughly. Sprinkle cornmeal over bottom of a 9-inch (23-cm) pie pan or dish. Spoon bean mixture over cornmeal in pan; set aside.

2　In a food processor or a large bowl, combine cottage cheese, butter, egg, apple-sauce, cumin, and salt. Whirl or beat with an electric mixer until smoothly puréed. Add flour; whirl or stir with a fork until dough holds together (dough will be sticky and soft). Scrape dough out onto a heavily floured board; with floured fingers, pat into a ball. Then, still using floured fingers, pat pastry into a 10-inch (25-cm) round. With a floured cookie cutter, cut one or more shapes (*each* 1 to 2 inches/2.5 to 5 cm in diameter) from center of pastry. Set cutouts aside.

3　Carefully lift pastry and place over filling in pie pan. Fold edge under to make it flush with pan rim; flute firmly against rim. Arrange cutouts decoratively atop pastry. Set pie in a shallow 10- by 15-inch (25- by 38-cm) baking pan. Brush pastry (including cutouts) with milk.

4　Bake on lowest rack of a 400°F (205°C) oven until pastry is well browned and filling is hot in center (about 1 hour). If pastry rim or cutouts begin to darken excessively before center of pastry is brown, drape rim and cover cutouts with foil. To serve, spoon filling and crust from dish. Makes 6 servings.

Per serving: *405 calories (29% calories from fat), 13 g total fat, 7 g saturated fat, 65 mg cholesterol, 463 mg sodium, 58 g carbohydrates, 4 g fiber, 15 g protein, 89 mg calcium, 4 mg iron*

Beer-braised Beans

Crumb Topping:

4   slices sourdough sandwich bread, torn into pieces

1   tablespoon (15 ml) olive oil

3   or 4 cloves garlic, minced

Beer-braised Beans:

1   large onion, chopped

2   cans (about 15 oz./425 g *each*) pinto beans, drained and rinsed

1   can (about 8 oz./230 g) tomato sauce

1   can (about 6 oz./170 g) tomato paste

½   cup (120 ml) beer (or to taste)

¼   cup (55 g) firmly packed brown sugar

3   tablespoons (45 ml) molasses

1½ teaspoons dry mustard

1½ teaspoons Worcestershire or reduced-sodium soy sauce

2   medium-size tomatoes (about 12 oz./340 g *total*), chopped

¾   cup (180 ml) nonfat sour cream

Sprinkled with garlic-seasoned bread crumbs and flavored with molasses, hot mustard, and a hint of beer, this dish goes together quickly for a satisfying meal. (Strict vegetarians may want to use soy sauce instead of Worcestershire.)

Preparation time: 25 minutes   **Cooking time:** About 25 minutes

1   In a blender or food processor, whirl bread to make fine crumbs. Pour crumbs into a wide nonstick frying pan and add oil and garlic. Cook over medium heat, stirring often, until crumbs are crisp and golden (about 15 minutes). Remove from pan and set aside. If made ahead, let cool completely; then store airtight until next day.

2   While crumbs are toasting, combine onion and ¼ cup (60 ml) water in a 3- to 4-quart (2.8- to 3.8- liter) pan. Cook over medium-high heat, stirring often, until onion is soft (about 5 minutes); add water, 1 tablespoon (15 ml) at a time, if pan appears dry. Stir in beans, tomato sauce, tomato paste, ¼ cup (60 ml) of the beer, sugar, molasses, mustard, and Worcestershire. Bring to a boil; then reduce heat so beans boil gently. Cook, uncovered, stirring occasionally, until flavors are blended (about 10 minutes). Add tomatoes and cook, stirring, just until heated through (about 3 minutes). Then remove from heat and stir in remaining ¼ cup (60 ml) beer.

3   Spoon beans into 4 wide individual bowls and sprinkle evenly with crumbs. Offer sour cream to add to taste. Makes 4 servings.

Per serving: *461 calories (12% calories from fat), 6 g total fat, 0.8 g saturated fat, 0 mg cholesterol, 1,268 mg sodium, 84 g carbohydrates, 11 g fiber, 18 g protein, 209 mg calcium, 6 mg iron*

Black Bean Hummus & Carrot Slaw Sandwiches

2   cans (about 15 oz./425 g *each*) black beans, drained and rinsed well

⅓   cup (45 g) finely chopped salted roasted almonds

¼   cup (60 ml) lemon juice

1   clove garlic, minced or pressed

½   teaspoon ground cumin

1½ pounds (680 g) carrots, shredded

1   teaspoon grated lime peel

⅓   cup (80 ml) lime juice

2   tablespoons (30 ml) distilled white vinegar

2   tablespoons (30 ml) honey

1   tablespoon (15 ml) Dijon mustard

1   teaspoon caraway seeds

¼   teaspoon crushed red pepper flakes

4   pita breads (*each* about 5 inches/12.5 cm in diameter)

1   large can (about 7 oz./200 g) whole green chiles, cut crosswise into halves

For a different take on a Mediterranean specialty, try making hummus with black beans and salted roasted almonds in place of the traditional garbanzos and sesame tahini. Serve the spread in pita breads, along with spoonfuls of tart-sweet carrot slaw for crunch and sparkling color.

Preparation time: 25 minutes

1   In a large bowl, combine beans, almonds, lemon juice, garlic, and cumin. Mash with a potato masher or fork until hummus has a spreadable consistency.

2   In another bowl, combine carrots, lime peel, lime juice, vinegar, honey, mustard, caraway seeds, and red pepper flakes. Mix well.

3   To serve, cut pita breads in half crosswise. Fill breads with hummus, carrot slaw (serve slaw with a slotted spoon), and chiles. Makes 4 servings.

Per serving: *489 calories (17% calories from fat), 10 g total fat, 0.9 g saturated fat, 0 mg cholesterol, 1,220 mg sodium, 86 g carbohydrates, 14 g fiber, 18 g protein, 181 mg calcium, 6 mg iron*

Mabu Tofu

1⅓ cups (247 g) long-grain white rice

1 package (about 1 lb./455 g) firm reduced-fat tofu, rinsed and drained

6 medium-size dried shiitake mushrooms (about ⅓ oz./10 g *total*)

8 green onions

2 teaspoons salad oil

1 pound (455 g) broccoli flowerets (about 7 cups)

½ cup (120 ml) sake

¼ cup (60 ml) reduced-sodium soy sauce

1 tablespoon sugar

1 teaspoon finely chopped fresh ginger

½ teaspoon pepper

2 teaspoons cornstarch blended with 1 tablespoon (15 ml) cold water

Meaty shiitake mushrooms add interest to a simple, sake-sauced stir-fry of tofu and broccoli. Alongside, you might offer whole tangerines to peel at the table.

Preparation time: 25 minutes   **Cooking time:** About 25 minutes

1 In a 3½- to 4-quart (3.3- to 3.8-liter) pan, bring 3 cups (710 ml) water to a boil over high heat; stir in rice. Reduce heat, cover, and simmer until liquid has been absorbed and rice is tender to bite (about 20 minutes).

2 Meanwhile, cut tofu into ½-inch (1-cm) chunks; place on paper towels and let drain for 10 minutes. Also, in a small bowl, combine mushrooms and 1 cup (240 ml) boiling water; let stand until mushrooms are softened (about 10 minutes). Lift mushrooms from water (reserve water); holding mushrooms over bowl, squeeze dry. Cut off and discard mushroom stems; then thinly slice caps and return to soaking water.

3 Thinly slice onions, keeping white and green parts separate. Heat oil in a wide nonstick frying pan over medium-high heat. Add broccoli and white part of onions; cook, stirring, for 1 minute. Add mushrooms and their soaking water; cover and cook, stirring occasionally, for 3 minutes. Add sake, soy sauce, sugar, ginger, pepper, and cornstarch mixture; bring to a boil, stirring. Add tofu, reduce heat, and simmer, stirring occasionally, until heated through (about 3 minutes).

4 To serve, spoon rice onto a platter or individual plates; top with tofu mixture and green part of onions. Makes 4 servings.

Per serving: *446 calories (14% calories from fat), 7 g total fat, 1 g saturated fat, 0 mg cholesterol, 676 mg sodium, 76 g carbohydrates, 5 g fiber, 19 g protein, 132 mg calcium, 5 mg iron*

Spicy Tofu Bok Choy

1⅓ cups (247 g) long-grain white rice

1 package (about 1 lb./455 g) firm reduced-fat tofu, rinsed and drained

1½ pounds (680 g) baby bok choy

1 tablespoon (15 ml) salad oil

3 cloves garlic, minced or pressed

8 green onions, thinly sliced

2 large red bell peppers (about 1 lb./455 g *total*), seeded and thinly sliced

6 tablespoons (90 ml) reduced-sodium soy sauce

4 teaspoons sugar

1 teaspoon liquid hot pepper seasoning (or to taste)

2 teaspoons cornstarch blended with 2 tablespoons (30 ml) cold water

Tofu is mild by nature—but it doesn't stay that way here! Garlic, hot pepper seasoning, and soy sauce enliven a combination of firm tofu, bok choy, and bell pepper. Serve over plenty of hot, fluffy rice.

Preparation time: 25 minutes   **Cooking time:** About 25 minutes

1 Cook rice as directed above for Mabu Tofu. Meanwhile, cut tofu into 1-inch (2.5-cm) slices. Place slices on paper towels and cover with more paper towels. Then set a flat pan on top layer of towels; set a 1-pound (455-g) can on pan. Let tofu drain for 10 minutes. While tofu is draining, cut each bok choy in half lengthwise; if any bok choy half is thicker than 1 inch (2.5 cm) at the base, cut it in half lengthwise. Set aside.

2 Cut tofu into 1-inch (2.5-cm) cubes. Heat oil in a wide nonstick frying pan over medium-high heat. Add tofu and cook, turning gently, until golden brown (about 5 minutes). With a slotted spoon, transfer tofu to paper towels to drain.

3 Add bok choy, garlic, onions, bell peppers, and ¼ cup (60 ml) water to pan. Cover and cook, stirring often, until bok choy stems are just tender when pierced (about 3 minutes). Uncover pan and add tofu, soy sauce, sugar, hot pepper seasoning, and cornstarch mixture; bring to a boil, stirring gently.

4 To serve, spoon rice onto a platter or individual plates; spoon tofu mixture over rice. Makes 4 servings.

Per serving: *438 calories (12% calories from fat), 6 g total fat, 1 g saturated fat, 0 mg cholesterol, 1,149 mg sodium, 79 g carbohydrates, 5 g fiber, 18 g protein, 281 mg calcium, 6 mg iron*

Maple-glazed Tofu in Acorn Squash *(Pictured on facing page)*

2 medium-size acorn squash (about 3½ lbs./1.6 kg *total*)

1½ cups (360 ml) vegetable broth

½ cup (45 g) dried cranberries or raisins

¼ cup (60 ml) pure maple syrup

2 large Granny Smith or Newtown Pippin apples (about 1 lb./455 g *total*)

1 tablespoon (15 ml) lemon juice

¾ teaspoon ground cinnamon

⅛ teaspoon ground nutmeg

1 tablespoon chopped walnuts

1 package (about 14 oz./400 g) firm tofu, rinsed, drained, and cut into ½-inch (1-cm) cubes

1 tablespoon (15 ml) balsamic vinegar

1 teaspoon cornstarch

⅓ cup (35 g) thinly sliced green onions

½ cup (120 ml) nonfat sour cream

Tender apple slices, rosy cranberries, and mild tofu, all cloaked in a savory-sweet maple sauce, are served in edible squash bowls for a wholesome and appealing main course. For the best flavor, use pure maple syrup rather than a maple-flavored variety.

Preparation time: 20 minutes   **Cooking time:** About 1 hour

1 Cut each squash in half lengthwise; scoop out and discard seeds and fibers. Place squash halves, cut side down, in a 9- by 13-inch (23- by 33-cm) baking pan. Add broth. Bake in a 350°F (175°C) oven until squash is tender when pierced (about 1 hour).

2 Meanwhile, in a small bowl, combine cranberries and syrup. Let stand until cranberries are softened (about 10 minutes), stirring occasionally. Also peel, core, and thinly slice apples; place in a large bowl, add lemon juice, and gently turn apples to coat with juice. Stir in cinnamon and nutmeg; set aside.

3 Toast walnuts in a wide nonstick frying pan over medium heat, stirring often, until golden (about 3 minutes). Remove from pan and set aside.

4 In frying pan, combine apples, cranberry mixture, and ¼ cup (60 ml) water. Cook over medium-high heat, stirring gently, until apples are almost tender when pierced (about 3 minutes). Add tofu and cook just until heated through (about 2 more minutes). In a small bowl, smoothly blend vinegar and cornstarch; add to tofu mixture. Cook, stirring, until sauce boils and thickens slightly (about 2 minutes). Remove from heat and stir in onions.

5 Arrange each squash half, skin side down, in a shallow individual bowl. Fill squash halves equally with tofu mixture; top with sour cream and sprinkle with walnuts. Makes 4 servings.

Per serving: *463 calories (20% calories from fat), 11 g total fat, 1 g saturated fat, 0 mg cholesterol, 421 mg sodium, 79 g carbohydrates, 14 g fiber, 21 g protein, 371 mg calcium, 13 mg iron*

Maple-glazed Tofu in Acorn Squash
(recipe on facing page)

Chocolate-crusted Cheesecake with Raspberries

Preparation time: *20 minutes, plus at least 4 hours to chill*

Cooking time: *About 55 minutes*

20 chocolate or honey graham crackers (*each* about 2 inches/5 cm square), finely crushed (about 1⅔ cups/140 g crumbs)

¼ cup (60 ml) raspberry jelly, melted

1 jar (about 7 oz./200 g) marshmallow fluff

1 cup (240 ml) low-fat (2%) cottage cheese

2 large packages (about 8 oz./230 g *each*) nonfat cream cheese, cut into chunks

3 tablespoons all-purpose flour

2 large eggs

2 teaspoons vanilla

1 cup (240 ml) nonfat sour cream

2 teaspoons berry-flavored liqueur (or to taste)

1 to 2 teaspoons sugar
Mint sprigs

2 cups (246 g) fresh raspberries or other fresh berries

In a small bowl, stir together graham cracker crumbs and jelly until well combined. Press firmly over bottom of a 9-inch (23-cm) cheesecake pan with a removable rim. Bake in a 350°F (175°C) oven for 10 minutes. Let cool on a rack for at least 5 minutes.

In a food processor or blender, whirl marshmallow fluff and cottage cheese until very smoothly puréed, scraping sides of container often. Add cream cheese; whirl until smoothly puréed, scraping sides of

Desserts
✳

container as needed. Add flour, eggs, and vanilla; whirl until smooth.

Pour filling evenly over crust. Bake in a 350°F (175°C) oven until top of cheesecake feels dry when lightly touched and center jiggles only slightly when pan is gently shaken (about 45 minutes). Remove from oven and carefully run a thin knife around pan rim. Let cool on a rack.

When cake is cool, combine sour cream, liqueur, and sugar in a small bowl. Beat just until blended. Spread over cake and smooth top. Cover and refrigerate until cold (at least 4 hours) or for up to 8 hours. Garnish with mint sprigs.

To serve, cut into slices and top with raspberries. Makes 10 to 12 servings.

Per serving: *275 calories (19% calories from fat), 6 g total fat, 0.5 g saturated fat, 45 mg cholesterol, 359 mg sodium, 41 g carbohydrates, 1 g fiber, 13 g protein, 169 mg calcium, 1 mg iron*

Nectarine Pudding

Preparation time: *20 minutes*
Cooking time: *About 45 minutes*

6 medium-size nectarines (about 1½ lbs./680 g *total*), pitted and quartered

1 tablespoon (15 ml) lemon juice

1 cup (240 ml) low-fat (2%) cottage cheese

⅓ cup (80 ml) half-and-half

1 cup (240 ml) low-fat (2%) milk

½ cup (100 g) sugar

1 large egg

2 large egg whites

1 teaspoon vanilla

½ cup (60 g) all-purpose flour

1 teaspoon ground cinnamon

1 cup (240 ml) pure maple syrup

1 teaspoon finely shredded lemon peel

In a large bowl, combine nectarines and lemon juice; turn fruit to coat with juice. Arrange nectarines attractively in a greased shallow 2½-quart (2.4-liter) casserole; set aside.

In a food processor or blender, whirl cottage cheese and half-and-half until smoothly puréed. Add milk, sugar, egg, egg whites, and vanilla. Whirl until smooth. Add flour and cinnamon; whirl just until evenly combined.

Carefully pour batter over nectarines. Bake in the top third of a 425°F (220°C) oven until top of pudding is golden brown and center jiggles only slightly when casserole is gently shaken (about 45 minutes). Let stand for about 5 minutes before serving.

Meanwhile, in a 1- to 1½-quart (950-ml to 1.4-liter) pan, combine syrup and lemon peel. Cook over medium heat, stirring, just until hot.

To serve, spoon pudding into bowls and top with hot maple sauce. Makes 6 servings.

Per serving: 384 calories (10% calories from fat), 5 g total fat, 2 g saturated fat, 47 mg cholesterol, 213 mg sodium, 77 g carbohydrates, 2 g fiber, 11 g protein, 141 mg calcium, 2 mg iron

✳

Chocolate-Banana Cake

Preparation time: *25 minutes*
Cooking time: *50 to 60 minutes*

1½ cups (185 g) all-purpose flour
½ cup (43 g) unsweetened cocoa
1 tablespoon baking powder
1½ teaspoons baking soda
½ teaspoon instant espresso powder or ¾ teaspoon instant coffee powder
1½ cups (330 g) firmly packed brown sugar
8 ounces (230 g) soft tofu, rinsed and drained
1 cup mashed ripe bananas
2 large egg whites
2 teaspoons vanilla
1 cup (100 g) sifted powdered sugar
   Mint sprigs

In a small bowl, stir together flour, cocoa, baking powder, baking soda, and espresso powder. Set aside. In a food processor or a large bowl, combine brown sugar, tofu, bananas, egg whites, and vanilla; whirl or beat with an electric mixer until smoothly blended. Add flour mixture; whirl or beat until well blended.

Spoon batter evenly into a well-greased, floured 3- to 3½-quart (2.8-

to 3.3-liter) fluted tube pan; smooth top. Bake in a 350°F (175°C) oven until top of cake springs back when gently pressed and sides begin to pull away from pan (50 to 60 minutes).

Let cake cool in pan on a rack for about 15 minutes. Carefully slide a thin knife between edge of cake and pan to loosen cake; then carefully invert cake onto rack, lift off pan, and let cool completely.

In a small bowl, stir together powdered sugar and 3 to 4 teaspoons (15 to 20 ml) water, or enough to make a glaze that is easy to drizzle; then drizzle glaze evenly over cooled cake. Garnish with mint sprigs. Makes 10 to 12 servings.

Per serving: 256 calories (4% calories from fat), 1 g total fat, 0.4 g saturated fat, 0 mg cholesterol, 329 mg sodium, 59 g carbohydrates, 2 g fiber, 4 g protein, 114 mg calcium, 2 mg iron

✳

Cinnamon Bread Pudding with Pumpkin Custard

Preparation time: *20 minutes*
Cooking time: *About 30 minutes*

¾ cup (110 g) raisins
8 to 10 ounces (230 to 280 g) unsliced day-old crusty sourdough bread
¼ cup (55 g) butter or margarine, melted
¾ cup (150 g) sugar
2 teaspoons ground cinnamon
3 large eggs
2¾ cups (650 ml) low-fat (2%) milk
1 can (about 1 lb./455 g) pumpkin
½ teaspoon ground nutmeg
1 teaspoon vanilla

In a small bowl, combine raisins and ¾ cup (180 ml) hot water; let stand until raisins are softened (about 10 minutes), stirring occasionally.

Meanwhile, tear bread into about 1-inch (2.5-cm) chunks; you should have about 6 cups. Place bread in a large bowl and mix in butter. In a small bowl, combine ¼ cup (50 g) of the sugar with cinnamon; sprinkle over bread, then mix gently but thoroughly. In another small bowl, beat one of the eggs with ¾ cup (180 ml) of the milk until blended; gently mix into bread mixture. Drain raisins well; add to bread mixture and mix just until evenly distributed.

Spoon bread mixture into a greased shallow 1½- to 2-quart (1.4- to 1.9-liter) baking dish. Bake in a 375°F (190°C) oven until crisp and deep brown (about 30 minutes).

Meanwhile, in the top of a 2- to 3-quart (1.9- to 2.8-liter) double boiler, combine remaining ½ cup (100 g) sugar, remaining 2 eggs, remaining 2 cups (470 ml) milk, pumpkin, nutmeg, and vanilla. Beat until blended. Then set over simmering water and cook, stirring often, until custard is steaming and thickly coats a metal spoon (about 12 minutes). Keep warm.

To serve, pour custard into individual bowls; spoon warm bread pudding on top. Makes 6 servings.

Per serving: 466 calories (28% calories from fat), 15 g total fat, 7 g saturated fat, 136 mg cholesterol, 431 mg sodium, 74 g carbohydrates, 3 g fiber, 12 g protein, 221 mg calcium, 3 mg iron

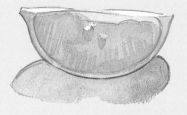

Mushroom & White Bean Pizza
(recipe on facing page)

Mushroom & White Bean Pizza *(Pictured on facing page)*

1 jar (about 6 oz./170 g) marinated quartered artichoke hearts

8 ounces (230 g) mushrooms, thinly sliced

4 cloves garlic, minced or pressed

3 tablespoons yellow cornmeal

2 cups (250 g) all-purpose flour

1 tablespoon baking powder

¼ teaspoon salt

¾ cup (180 ml) low-fat (2%) cottage cheese

1 tablespoon sugar

2 tablespoons (30 ml) *each* nonfat milk and olive oil

¾ cup (85 g) *each* shredded smoked Gouda and part-skim mozzarella cheese (or use all of one kind)

1 tablespoon chopped fresh oregano or 1 teaspoon dried oregano

1 can (about 15 oz./425 g) cannellini (white kidney beans), drained and rinsed

1 large firm-ripe pear-shaped (Roma-type) tomato (about 4 oz./115 g), very thinly sliced lengthwise

¼ cup (25 g) very thinly sliced red onion

About ⅛ teaspoon crushed red pepper flakes (or to taste)

Oregano sprigs (optional)

Our tender no-yeast pizza dough gets a pleasantly moist texture—and extra protein—from cottage cheese. The topping offers some delicious surprises: smoked Gouda cheese and mild, creamy-textured white beans join the familiar mushrooms and tomatoes.

Preparation time: 30 minutes   **Cooking time:** About 20 minutes

1 Drain artichokes well, reserving marinade; you should have ¼ cup (60 ml) marinade. (If necessary, add equal parts water and olive oil to marinade to make ¼ cup/60 ml liquid.) Set artichokes and marinade aside.

2 In a medium-size nonstick frying pan, combine mushrooms, garlic, and ¼ cup (60 ml) water. Cook over medium-high heat, stirring occasionally, until mushrooms are soft and almost all liquid has evaporated (about 7 minutes; do not scorch). Remove from pan and set aside.

3 Sprinkle cornmeal over bottom of a lightly greased 12-inch (30-cm) deep-dish pizza pan; set aside. In a medium-size bowl, stir together flour, baking powder, and salt; set aside.

4 In a food processor or a large bowl, combine cottage cheese, the reserved ¼ cup artichoke marinade, sugar, milk, and oil. Whirl or beat with an electric mixer until smoothly puréed. Add flour mixture; whirl or beat just until dough holds together. Turn dough out onto a lightly floured board and knead several times, or until dough holds together (dough will be soft). Then place dough in pizza pan. Flour your hands thoroughly; then flatten dough with the heels of your hands and your fingertips to cover pan bottom evenly. (Or roll dough on board into a 12½-inch/31-cm round and carefully fit into pan.)

5 Gently stretch edge of dough up sides of pan to form about a ½-inch (1-cm) rim. Prick dough all over with a fork; then sprinkle evenly with Gouda cheese, mozzarella cheese, and chopped oregano.

6 Arrange mushrooms, beans, artichokes, tomato, and onion over cheese. Bake pizza on middle rack of a 500°F (260°C) oven until crust is golden and cheese is melted (about 10 minutes). Sprinkle with red pepper flakes and garnish with oregano sprigs, if desired. Serve immediately. Makes 6 servings.

Per serving: *420 calories (29% calories from fat), 14 g total fat, 5 g saturated fat, 24 mg cholesterol, 855 mg sodium, 54 g carbohydrates, 5 g fiber, 21 g protein, 390 mg calcium, 4 mg iron*

White Bean Tagine

1 teaspoon sesame seeds

1 large onion, chopped

1½ cups (360 ml) low-fat (2%) milk

1 package (about 10 oz./285 g) couscous

2 cans (about 15 oz./425 g *each*) cannellini (white kidney beans), drained and rinsed

½ cup (120 ml) vegetable broth

3 tablespoons (45 ml) honey

¼ teaspoon *each* ground ginger and ground cinnamon

⅛ teaspoon ground saffron or a large pinch of saffron threads

⅛ teaspoon ground white pepper

6 apricots (about 12 oz./340 g *total*), pitted and quartered

⅓ cup (15 g) cilantro leaves
   Salt

Juicy fresh apricots add a tart and surprising accent to this vegetarian version of a sweet-spiced Moroccan-style stew.

Preparation time: 15 minutes   **Cooking time:** About 20 minutes

1 Toast sesame seeds in a wide nonstick frying pan over medium heat, stirring often, until golden (about 3 minutes). Remove from pan and set aside.

2 In same pan, combine onion and ¼ cup (60 ml) water. Cook over medium-high heat, stirring often, until onion is soft (about 5 minutes); add water, 1 tablespoon (15 ml) at a time, if pan appears dry. Remove from heat.

3 In a 2- to 3-quart (1.9- to 2.8-liter) pan, bring milk and 1 cup (240 ml) water just to a boil over medium-high heat. Stir in couscous; cover, remove from heat, and let stand until liquid has been absorbed (about 5 minutes). Keep warm; fluff occasionally with a fork.

4 Meanwhile, to onion mixture, add beans, broth, honey, ginger, cinnamon, saffron, and white pepper. Bring to a boil over medium-high heat. Then reduce heat so mixture boils gently; cook, stirring occasionally, for 5 minutes. Add apricots; cook, stirring gently, just until heated through (about 3 minutes).

5 To serve, spoon couscous onto a rimmed platter; top with bean mixture. Sprinkle with cilantro and sesame seeds; season to taste with salt. Makes 4 servings.

Per serving: *578 calories (7% calories from fat), 4 g total fat, 1 g saturated fat, 7 mg cholesterol, 445 mg sodium, 111 g carbohydrates, 13 g fiber, 25 g protein, 210 mg calcium, 4 mg iron*

Minted Lentils & Cabbage with Feta

1¾ cups (350 g) lentils

3 cups (710 ml) vegetable broth

1 teaspoon dried oregano

⅓ cup (80 ml) lemon juice

2 tablespoons (30 ml) olive oil

1 to 2 teaspoons honey

⅛ teaspoon *each* salt and pepper

1 small head red cabbage (about 1 lb./455 g)

1 teaspoon olive oil

1 small red onion (about 6 oz./170 g), finely chopped

1 or 2 cloves garlic, minced or pressed

3 tablespoons chopped fresh mint or about ½ teaspoon dried mint

½ cup (65 g) crumbled feta cheese

Tender lentils and shredded red cabbage, flavored with lemon and mint and topped with feta cheese, make a tempting and colorful meatless entrée.

Preparation time: 20 minutes   **Cooking time:** About 35 minutes

1 Sort through lentils, discarding any debris. Rinse and drain lentils. In a 2- to 3-quart (1.9- to 2.8-liter) pan, bring broth to a boil over high heat. Add lentils and oregano. Reduce heat, cover, and simmer until lentils are tender to bite (about 25 minutes). Drain and discard any remaining cooking liquid; keep lentils warm.

2 While lentils are simmering, beat together lemon juice, the 2 tablespoons oil, honey, salt, and pepper in a small bowl. Set aside. Also remove 5 to 7 large outer leaves from cabbage. Use leaves to line a large serving bowl; set aside. Core remaining cabbage and finely shred to make 5 cups (350 g); set aside.

3 Heat the 1 teaspoon oil in a wide nonstick frying pan over medium-high heat. Add onion and cook, stirring often, just until soft (about 4 minutes); add water, 1 tablespoon (15 ml) at a time, if pan appears dry. Add half the shredded cabbage, 1 tablespoon (15 ml) water, and garlic; cook, stirring, until cabbage just begins to wilt. Then add remaining shredded cabbage and 1 tablespoon (15 ml) more water; cook, stirring, until all cabbage is wilted (2 to 3 more minutes).

4 Remove cabbage mixture from heat and gently stir in lentils and mint. Then spoon lentil-cabbage mixture into serving bowl and sprinkle with cheese. Stir lemon juice mixture and drizzle over salad. Makes 6 to 8 servings.

Per serving: *274 calories (24% calories from fat), 8 g total fat, 2 g saturated fat, 9 mg cholesterol, 592 mg sodium, 38 g carbohydrates, 7 g fiber, 16 g protein, 119 mg calcium, 5 mg iron*

Yellow Split Pea Dal with Brown Rice & Broccoli

1 cup (200 g) yellow split peas

About 5½ cups (1.3 liters) vegetable broth

2 large onions, chopped

2 medium-size carrots (about 8 oz./230 g *total*), diced

2 tablespoons finely chopped fresh ginger

2 large cloves garlic, minced or pressed

2 teaspoons *each* ground turmeric and chili powder

1 large can (about 28 oz./795 g) crushed tomatoes

1 pound (455 g) butternut or other gold-fleshed squash, peeled and cut into ¾-inch (2-cm) cubes

2 cups (370 g) long-grain brown rice

3 cups (200 g) broccoli flowerets

½ cup (20 g) cilantro leaves

About 1½ cups (240 ml) plain nonfat yogurt

Lime wedges

Crushed red pepper flakes

Salt

Dal is a spicy Indian dish based on dried legumes; this one features yellow split peas, curry seasonings, and an abundance of fresh vegetables. It does take several hours to cook, so plan to serve it on a day when you can afford to spend some time in the kitchen.

Preparation time: 30 minutes   **Cooking time:** About 2½ hours

1 Sort through peas, discarding any debris; then rinse peas, drain, and set aside.

2 In a 6- to 8-quart (6- to 8-liter) pan, combine 1 cup (240 ml) of the broth, onions, carrots, ginger, and garlic. Cook over medium-high heat, stirring often, until liquid evaporates and browned bits stick to pan bottom (about 15 minutes). To deglaze pan, add ⅓ cup (80 ml) more broth, stirring to loosen browned bits from pan; continue to cook until browned bits form again. Repeat deglazing step about 3 more times or until vegetables are browned, using about ⅓ cup (80 ml) broth each time.

3 To vegetable mixture, add peas, turmeric, chili powder, tomatoes and their liquid, and 3 cups (710 ml) more broth. Bring to a boil; then reduce heat, cover, and simmer for 1 hour. Add squash; cover and simmer, stirring often, until squash is tender to bite (40 to 50 more minutes).

4 Meanwhile, in a 5- to 6-quart (5- to 6-liter) pan, bring 4 cups (950 ml) water to a boil over high heat; stir in rice. Reduce heat, cover, and simmer until liquid has been absorbed and rice is tender to bite (about 45 minutes). Remove from pan and keep warm; fluff occasionally with a fork.

5 Wash pan and add broccoli and ⅓ cup (80 ml) water. Cover and cook over medium-high heat until broccoli is almost tender-crisp to bite (about 3 minutes). Uncover and continue to cook, stirring, until all liquid has evaporated.

6 To serve, spoon rice, broccoli, and split pea mixture onto individual plates. Offer cilantro, yogurt, lime, red pepper flakes, and salt to season each serving to taste. Makes 6 servings.

Per serving: *516 calories (7% calories from fat), 4 g total fat, 0.6 g saturated fat, 1 mg cholesterol, 1,445 mg sodium, 102 g carbohydrates, 10 g fiber, 22 g protein, 253 mg calcium, 5 mg iron*

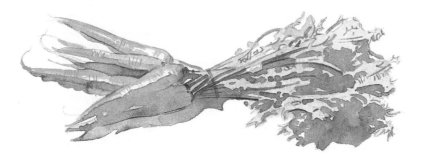

Lentil-Nut Shepherd's Pie

1½   cups (300 g) lentils

2   cloves garlic, minced or pressed

1½   teaspoons *each* dried thyme and dried savory

½   teaspoon dried rubbed sage

5½   cups (1.3 liters) vegetable broth

½   cup (65 g) chopped walnuts

2   cups (90 g) soft whole wheat bread crumbs

2   pounds (905 g) thin-skinned potatoes, peeled and cut into 2-inch (5-cm) chunks

1   cup (about 4 oz./115 g) shredded reduced-fat sharp Cheddar cheese

Like traditional shepherd's pie, this vegetarian rendition is topped with spoonfuls of mashed potato. The filling, though, omits the usual beef or lamb; instead, it's a combination of herb-seasoned lentils, walnuts, and whole wheat bread crumbs.

Preparation time: 15 minutes   **Cooking time:** About 1 hour and 10 minutes

1 Sort through lentils, discarding any debris. Rinse lentils, drain, and place in a 3- to 4-quart (2.8- to 3.8-liter) pan. Add garlic, thyme, savory, sage, and 3½ cups (830 ml) of the broth. Bring to a boil over high heat; then reduce heat, cover, and simmer until lentils are tender to bite (about 25 minutes). Remove from heat and stir in walnuts and bread crumbs.

2 While lentils are simmering, combine potatoes and remaining 2 cups (470 ml) broth in a 2- to 3-quart (1.9- to 2.8-liter) pan. Bring to a boil over high heat; then reduce heat, cover, and simmer until potatoes mash easily when pressed (15 to 20 minutes). Drain, reserving liquid. Leaving potatoes in pan, beat or mash them until smooth. Mix in ½ cup (120 ml) of the reserved liquid; then stir in cheese.

3 Stir remaining potato-cooking liquid into lentil mixture; spoon into a 9- by 13-inch (23- by 33-cm) baking pan. Drop potatoes in spoonfuls onto lentil mixture. Bake in a 375°F (190°C) oven until potatoes are golden brown (about 35 minutes). Makes 8 servings.

Per serving: *340 calories (23% calories from fat), 9 g total fat, 2 g saturated fat, 10 mg cholesterol, 874 mg sodium, 49 g carbohydrates, 7 g fiber, 19 g protein, 172 mg calcium, 5 mg iron*

Split Pea & Green Pea Salad   *(Pictured on facing page)*

1   cup (200 g) green split peas

2   cups (470 ml) vegetable broth

½   teaspoon dried thyme

1   package (about 10 oz./285 g) frozen tiny peas (do not thaw)

4   ounces/115 g (about 10 tablespoons) dried orzo or other rice-shaped pasta

¼   cup (25 g) thinly sliced green onions

¼   cup (10 g) chopped fresh mint

¼   cup (60 ml) salad oil

1   teaspoon finely shredded lemon peel

2   tablespoons (30 ml) lemon juice

     About 24 large butter lettuce leaves, rinsed and crisped

     Mint and thyme sprigs

     Salt and pepper

Dotted with sweet green peas, this simple split pea and pasta salad is seasoned with fresh mint and lemon. Don't thaw the green peas before you stir them into the salad; they'll help to cool the freshly cooked split peas quickly.

Preparation time: 15 minutes   **Cooking time:** About 30 minutes

1 Sort through split peas, discarding any debris; then rinse and drain peas. In a 1½- to 2-quart (1.4- to 1.9-liter) pan, bring broth to a boil over high heat. Add split peas and dried thyme. Reduce heat, cover, and simmer until split peas are tender to bite (about 25 minutes); drain and discard any remaining cooking liquid. Transfer split peas to a large bowl, add frozen peas, and mix gently but thoroughly. Let stand, stirring occasionally, until mixture is cool (about 3 minutes).

2 Meanwhile, in a 4- to 5-quart (3.8- to 5-liter) pan, bring about 8 cups (1.9 liters) water to a boil over medium-high heat; stir in pasta and cook until just tender to bite, about 5 minutes. (Or cook pasta according to package directions.) Drain, rinse with cold water, and drain well again. Transfer pasta to bowl with peas. Add onions and chopped mint; mix gently. In a small bowl, beat oil, lemon peel, and lemon juice until blended. Add to pea mixture; mix gently but thoroughly. If made ahead, cover and refrigerate for up to 3 hours.

3 To serve, line 4 individual plates with lettuce leaves; top each plate equally with pea mixture. Garnish with mint and thyme sprigs. Season to taste with salt and pepper. Makes 4 servings.

Per serving: *458 calories (30% calories from fat), 15 g total fat, 2 g saturated fat, 0 mg cholesterol, 607 mg sodium, 62 g carbohydrates, 6 g fiber, 19 g protein, 56 mg calcium, 2 mg iron*

Split Pea & Green Pea Salad
(recipe on facing page)

Baked Lentils with Honey & Chutney

Preparation time: *15 minutes*
Cooking time: *1 to 1¼ hours*

1¾ cups (350 g) lentils
6 slices (115 g) bacon, chopped; or 1 tablespoon (15 ml) salad oil
¾ cup (75 g) sliced green onions
⅓ cup (80 ml) *each* honey and chopped Major Grey's chutney
2 teaspoons dry mustard
    Lime wedges
    Salt and pepper

Sort through lentils, discarding any debris. Rinse lentils, drain.

Cook bacon in a 3- to 4-quart (2.8- to 3.8-liter) pan over medium-high heat until crisp; drain on paper towels. Pour off and discard all but 1 tablespoon (15 ml) drippings from pan (or discard all drippings and add oil to pan).

Reserve 2 tablespoons of the onions; add remaining onions to pan. Cook, stirring often, until soft (about 5 minutes). Add lentils and 4 cups (950 ml) water. Bring to a boil over high heat; then reduce heat, cover, and simmer for 20 minutes. Stir in honey, chutney, and mustard.

Pour mixture into a shallow 2-quart (1.9-liter) casserole. Bake in a 350°F (175°C) oven, stirring several times, until almost all liquid has been absorbed (35 to 45 minutes). Mix in bacon and sprinkle with the reserved 2 tablespoons onions. Garnish with lime wedges; season to taste with salt and pepper. Makes 6 servings.

Per serving: *345 calories (13% calories from fat), 5 g total fat, 2 g saturated fat, 6 mg cholesterol, 259 mg sodium, 59 g carbohydrates, 7 g fiber, 18 g protein, 41 mg calcium, 5 mg iron*

Almost Vegetarian Legume Dishes

✳

Stir-fried Broccoli & Black Beans with Pork

Preparation time: *25 minutes*
Cooking time: *About 30 minutes*

1 package (about ½ oz./15 g) dried shiitake mushrooms
1 cup (185 g) long-grain white rice
1 medium-size head garlic (about 3 oz./85 g), separated into cloves
2 teaspoons salad oil
5 cups (325 g) broccoli flowerets
1 can (about 15 oz./425 g) black beans, drained and rinsed well
4 to 8 ounces (115 to 230 g) Chinese-style barbecued pork (or use leftover roast pork), cut into thin ½-inch (1-cm) squares
2 tablespoons (30 ml) reduced-sodium soy sauce
1 teaspoon Oriental sesame oil
½ teaspoon honey

Place mushrooms in a small bowl and add enough boiling water to cover; let stand until mushrooms are softened (about 10 minutes). Lift mushrooms from water and squeeze dry; discard water. Trim and discard mushroom stems; then thinly slice caps. Set aside in a small bowl.

While mushrooms are soaking, bring 2 cups (470 ml) water to a boil in a 3- to 4-quart (2.8- to 3.8-liter) pan over high heat; stir in rice. Reduce heat, cover, and simmer until liquid has been absorbed and rice is tender to bite (about 20 minutes). Transfer to a rimmed platter and keep warm; fluff occasionally with a fork.

Peel and thinly slice garlic cloves. Heat salad oil in a wide nonstick frying pan over medium-high heat. Add garlic and cook, stirring, just until tinged with brown (about 2 minutes; do not scorch). Add water, 1 tablespoon (15 ml) at a time, if pan appears dry. Remove garlic from pan with a slotted spoon and place in bowl with mushrooms. Add broccoli and ⅓ cup (80 ml) water to pan. Cover and cook until broccoli is almost tender-crisp to bite (about 3 minutes). Uncover and cook, stirring, until liquid has evaporated. Add beans and pork; cook, stirring often, until heated through.

Remove pan from heat and add mushroom mixture, soy sauce, sesame oil, and honey; mix gently but thoroughly. Spoon broccoli mixture over rice. Makes 4 servings.

Per serving: *460 calories (16% calories from fat), 9 g total fat, 2 g saturated fat, 34 mg cholesterol, 587 mg sodium, 71 g carbohydrates, 9 g fiber, 32 g protein, 149 mg calcium, 5 mg iron*

Light Cassoulet

Preparation time: *30 minutes*
Cooking time: *About 1½ hours*

1   large onion, chopped

2   medium-size carrots (about 8 oz./230 g *total*), thinly sliced

1   medium-size red bell pepper (about 6 oz./170 g), seeded and thinly sliced

3   cloves garlic, minced or pressed

1   can (about 14½ oz./415 g) low-sodium stewed tomatoes

1¾ cups (420 ml) vegetable broth

⅔   cup (160 ml) dry red wine

1   teaspoon dried thyme

1   dried bay leaf

¼   teaspoon *each* pepper and liquid hot pepper seasoning

2   cans (about 15 oz./425 g *each*) cannellini (white kidney beans), drained and rinsed

1½ pounds (680 g) boneless, skinless chicken breasts, cut into 1-inch (2.5-cm) pieces

4   ounces (115 g) turkey kielbasa (Polish sausage), thinly sliced

¼   cup (15 g) finely chopped parsley

In a 5- to 6-quart (5- to 6-liter) pan, combine onion, carrots, bell pepper, garlic, and ½ cup (120 ml) water. Cook over medium-high heat, stirring often, until liquid evaporates and browned bits stick to pan bottom (about 10 minutes). To deglaze pan, add ⅓ cup (80 ml) water, stirring to loosen browned bits from pan; continue to cook until browned bits form again. Repeat deglazing step about 2 more times or until vegetables are browned, using ⅓ cup (80 ml) water each time. Stir in tomatoes and their liquid, broth, wine, thyme, bay leaf, pepper, and hot pepper seasoning. Bring to a boil; then reduce heat, cover, and simmer for 45 minutes.

Stir in beans; simmer, uncovered, for 10 minutes. Stir in chicken and sausage. Continue to simmer, uncovered, until chicken is no longer pink in center; cut to test (about 10 more minutes). Just before serving, remove and discard bay leaf. To serve, ladle mixture into bowls and sprinkle with parsley. Makes 8 servings.

Per serving: 240 calories (12% calories from fat), 3 g total fat, 1 g saturated fat, 59 mg cholesterol, 557 mg sodium, 24 g carbohydrates, 7 g fiber, 29 g protein, 75 mg calcium, 3 mg iron

Thai Pizza with Shrimp

Preparation time: *20 minutes*
Cooking time: *About 15 minutes*

6   small Italian bread shells (*each* about 5½ inches/13.5 cm in diameter and about 4 oz./115 g); or 6 pita breads (*each* about 5 inches/12.5 cm in diameter); or 6 English muffins, split

½   cup (120 ml) reduced-fat creamy peanut butter

3   tablespoons (45 ml) hoisin sauce

2   tablespoons (30 ml) seasoned rice vinegar (or 2 tablespoons/30 ml distilled white vinegar plus 1 teaspoon sugar)

1   teaspoon Oriental sesame oil

1   cup (170 g) bean sprouts

1   cup (about 4 oz./115 g) shredded reduced-fat jack cheese

5   to 6 ounces (140 to 170 g) small cooked shrimp

¼   cup (25 g) thinly sliced green onions

    Crushed red pepper flakes

Place bread shells, pita breads, or muffin halves (cut side up) on two 12- by 15-inch (30- by 38-cm) baking sheets.

In a bowl, combine peanut butter, hoisin sauce, vinegar, and sesame oil. Beat until smoothly blended; if necessary, add a little water so sauce is easy to spread. Spread equally over cupped area of bread shells or top of pita breads (or spread to edge of muffin halves). Scatter bean sprouts equally over sauce; sprinkle with cheese.

Bake in a 350°F (175°C) oven until cheese is melted and beginning to brown (12 to 15 minutes; if using one oven, switch positions of baking sheets after 7 minutes). Place each pizza on an individual plate,; top pizzas equally with shrimp and onions. Season to taste with red pepper flakes. Makes 6 servings.

Per serving: 410 calories (29% calories from fat), 13 g total fat, 4 g saturated fat, 62 mg cholesterol, 876 mg sodium, 50 g carbohydrates, 2 g fiber, 23 g protein, 233 mg calcium, 3 mg iron

Bruschetta with Tomato, Basil & Yogurt Cheese
(recipe on page 80)

Eggs & Cheese

You may think of egg and cheese dishes as perfect for meatless menus, but not so great for low-fat meals. If so, the recipes in this chapter should change your mind! Spinach Soufflé, Corn Custard, Chile-Cheese French Toast, Quick Fruit & Ricotta Pizza, Overnight Fiery Oven Strata—all are lean, wonderful choices for family meals as well as casual entertaining. And many work well at just about any time of day, offering delicious dining for brunch, lunch, or supper.

Bruschetta with Tomato, Basil & Yogurt Cheese *(Pictured on page 78)*

Yogurt Cheese:

4 cups (950 ml) plain nonfat yogurt

¼ cup (10 g) finely chopped fresh basil

Bruschetta:

½ cup (55 g) pine nuts

8 slices crusty bread (*each* about ½ inch / 1 cm thick; about 1 lb. / 455 g *total*), such as Italian ciabatta or French bread

1 cup (40 g) lightly packed fresh basil leaves

1 pound (455 g) pear-shaped (Roma-type) tomatoes, finely chopped

½ cup (40 g) grated Parmesan cheese

Garnish:

Basil sprigs (optional)

In Italy, bruschetta is thick-sliced bread that's grilled over charcoal and brushed with olive oil and garlic—and sometimes topped with tomatoes and seasonings. Here's a lean version to enjoy for lunch or a light dinner. Start by preparing a tangy, basil-seasoned yogurt cheese; then spread it thickly on toasted crusty bread and top with more fresh basil, tomatoes, and pine nuts.

Preparation time: 20 minutes, plus at least 12 hours to chill   **Cooking time:** About 8 minutes

1 To prepare yogurt cheese, line a fine strainer with a double layer of cheesecloth. Set strainer over a deep bowl (bottom of strainer should sit at least 2 inches / 5 cm above bottom of bowl). In a large bowl, stir together yogurt and chopped basil; then scrape mixture into cloth-lined strainer. Cover airtight and refrigerate until yogurt has the consistency of whipped cream cheese (at least 12 hours) or for up to 2 days; occasionally drain and discard liquid as it accumulates.

2 Toast pine nuts in a medium-size frying pan over medium heat, stirring often, until golden (about 3 minutes). Remove from pan and set aside.

3 Arrange bread slices slightly apart in a shallow 10- by 15-inch (25- by 38-cm) baking pan. Broil about 6 inches below heat, turning once, until golden on both sides (about 5 minutes). Let toast cool on a rack.

4 Top each toast slice with equal portions of yogurt cheese, basil leaves, tomatoes, pine nuts, and Parmesan cheese. Garnish with basil sprigs, if desired. Makes 8 servings.

Per serving: 279 calories (25% calories from fat), 8 g total fat, 2 g saturated fat, 5 mg cholesterol, 491 mg sodium, 39 g carbohydrates, 3 g fiber, 15 g protein, 347 mg calcium, 4 mg iron

Quick Fruit & Ricotta Pizza

1 package (about 10 oz. / 285 g) refrigerated pizza crust dough

1 cup (about 8 oz. / 230 g) part-skim ricotta cheese

2 teaspoons grated lemon peel

2 cups (about 8 oz. / 230 g) shredded part-skim mozzarella cheese

2 medium-size nectarines (about 8 oz. / 230 g *total*), pitted and thinly sliced

4 ounces (115 g) dried peaches, thinly sliced

¾ cup (130 g) halved red seedless grapes

2 tablespoons sugar

¼ teaspoon ground cinnamon

3 tablespoons sliced almonds

Take advantage of refrigerated dough for this quick main dish. Though not traditional for pizza, the toppings—fresh and dried fruits, ricotta and mozzarella cheeses, and cinnamon sugar—taste just right at breakfast time or for a weekend brunch.

Preparation time: 20 minutes   **Cooking time:** 15 to 20 minutes

1 Unroll dough, place on a 12- by 15-inch (30- by 38-cm) nonstick baking sheet, and press with your fingers to make a 10- by 15-inch (25- by 38-cm) rectangle. Bake on lowest rack of a 425°F (220°C) oven until browned (about 8 minutes). Remove from oven.

2 In a small bowl, stir together ricotta cheese and lemon peel; spread over crust. Sprinkle with mozzarella cheese. Arrange nectarines, peaches, and grapes over cheese. In another small bowl, mix sugar and cinnamon. Sprinkle sugar mixture and almonds evenly over fruit. Return to oven and bake until fruit is hot to the touch and mozzarella cheese is melted (5 to 10 minutes). Makes 8 servings.

Per serving: 287 calories (29% calories from fat), 9 g total fat, 5 g saturated fat, 25 mg cholesterol, 364 mg sodium, 36 g carbohydrates, 2 g fiber, 14 g protein, 274 mg calcium, 2 mg iron

Baked Quesadillas

1   can (about 15 oz./425 g) black beans, drained and rinsed well

¼   cup (60 ml) nonfat mayonnaise

2   teaspoons wine vinegar

1   teaspoon chili powder

4   nonfat flour tortillas (*each about 7 inches/18 cm in diameter*)

1   cup (about 4 oz./115 g) shredded reduced-fat jack or sharp Cheddar cheese

2   small firm-ripe pear-shaped (Roma-type) tomatoes (about 4 oz./115 g *total*), chopped

½   cup (85 g) chopped red onion

⅓   cup (15 g) cilantro leaves

½   cup (120 ml) purchased or homemade green tomatillo salsa

Quick and easy! To make this light dinner or lunch, fill tortillas with seasoned black beans, jack cheese, tomatoes, and red onion. Serve with tall glasses of lemonade and a selection of fresh fruit.

Preparation time: 15 minutes   **Cooking time:** About 7 minutes

1   In a medium-size bowl, coarsely mash beans. Add mayonnaise, vinegar, and chili powder; stir until well blended.

2   Lightly brush both sides of each tortilla with water. Spoon a fourth of the bean mixture over half of each tortilla; evenly sprinkle a fourth each of the cheese, tomatoes, onion, and cilantro over bean mixture on each tortilla. Fold plain half of tortilla over to cover filling.

3   Set quesadillas slightly apart on a lightly greased 12- by 15-inch (30- by 38-cm) baking sheet. Bake in a 500°F (260°C) oven until crisp and golden (about 7 minutes). Serve with salsa. Makes 4 servings.

Per serving: *250 calories (27% calories from fat), 8 g total fat, 4 g saturated fat, 20 mg cholesterol, 998 mg sodium, 30 g carbohydrates, 5 g fiber, 16 g protein, 381 mg calcium, 2 mg iron*

Egg & Potato Hash

2   large russet potatoes (about 1¼ lbs./565 g *total*), peeled and cut into ½-inch (1-cm) cubes

6   reduced-fat flour tortillas (*each about 7 inches/18 cm in diameter*)

1½   teaspoons Oriental sesame oil

3   medium-size onions, chopped

6   cloves garlic, minced or pressed

3   small fresh jalapeño chiles, seeded and finely chopped

⅔   cup (30 g) chopped cilantro

2   teaspoons ground cumin

3   tablespoons (45 ml) lime juice

8   large eggs, beaten to blend

About 1½ cups (360 ml) purchased or homemade salsa

Salt and pepper

Seasoned with jalapeño chiles and Oriental sesame oil, this wholesome hash draws its flavors from both East and West. Serve it with warm flour tortillas and your favorite salsa.

Preparation time: 25 minutes   **Cooking time:** About 20 minutes

1   Pour water into a 2- to 3-quart (1.9- to 2.8-liter) pan to a depth of 1 inch (2.5 cm). Add potatoes, cover, and bring to a boil over high heat; then reduce heat and simmer until potatoes are tender when pierced (10 to 12 minutes). Drain potatoes well.

2   While potatoes are simmering, sprinkle tortillas lightly with water; then stack tortillas, wrap in foil, and heat in a 350°F (175°C) oven until warm (10 to 12 minutes).

3   Meanwhile, heat oil in a wide nonstick frying pan over medium heat. Add onions and garlic. Cook, stirring often, until onions are soft (about 10 minutes); add water, 1 tablespoon (15 ml) at a time, if pan appears dry. Add chiles, cilantro, and cumin; cook, stirring often, for 1 to 2 minutes.

4   Add lime juice and drained potatoes to onion mixture in pan; then spread mixture out to make level. Pour beaten eggs over potatoes. Cook until eggs are set to your liking, using a wide spatula to lift cooked portion from pan bottom to allow uncooked eggs to flow underneath.

5   Spoon egg mixture onto plates; offer salsa, salt, and pepper to add to taste. Serve with tortillas. Makes 6 servings.

Per serving: *323 calories (29% calories from fat), 10 g total fat, 2 g saturated fat, 283 mg cholesterol, 1,028 mg sodium, 43 g carbohydrates, 4 g fiber, 14 g protein, 168 mg calcium, 3 mg iron*

Upside-down Pizza Pie *(Pictured on facing page)*

Filling:

1   cup (240 ml) low-fat (2%) cottage cheese

¼   cup (10 g) fresh basil leaves

1   tablespoon grated Parmesan cheese

2   or 3 cloves garlic, minced or pressed

1   teaspoon Oriental sesame oil

½   cup (69 g) yellow cornmeal

1   teaspoon olive oil

8   ounces (230 g) mushrooms, thinly sliced

1   large onion, chopped

½   teaspoon dried thyme

1   large jar (about 14 oz./400 g) roasted red peppers, drained and rinsed

1   cup (about 4 oz./115 g) shredded part-skim mozzarella cheese

¼   teaspoon *each* dried rubbed sage and dried marjoram

1   large tomato (about 8 oz./ 230 g), very thinly sliced

Batter Topping:

1⅓   cups (165 g) all-purpose flour

⅓   cup (45 g) yellow cornmeal

1   tablespoon sugar

1½   teaspoons baking powder

¼   to ½ teaspoon dried oregano

¼   teaspoon salt

½   cup (120 ml) nonfat milk

2   tablespoons (30 ml) olive oil

2   large egg whites

Pizza en casserole? It may sound a bit strange, but it's delicious! Layers of favorite pizza toppings—mushrooms, onions, red peppers, tomatoes, and cheese—are topped with a cornmeal batter, then baked. Accompany the dish with a crisp green salad.

Preparation time: 30 minutes   **Cooking time:** About 45 minutes

1 In a blender or food processor, combine cottage cheese, basil, Parmesan cheese, garlic, and sesame oil. Whirl until smoothly puréed; set aside. Sprinkle the ½ cup (69 g) cornmeal evenly over bottom of a greased deep 2½- to 3-quart (2.4- to 2.8-liter) casserole; set aside.

2 Heat the 1 teaspoon olive oil in a wide nonstick frying pan over medium-high heat. Add mushrooms, onion, thyme, and ¼ cup (60 ml) water. Cook, stirring occasionally, until vegetables are soft and almost all liquid has evaporated (about 10 minutes).

3 Spoon vegetable mixture over cornmeal in casserole. Top evenly with cottage cheese mixture, spreading to smooth top. Cover cottage cheese layer with red peppers, overlapping if necessary; sprinkle peppers evenly with mozzarella cheese, sage, and marjoram. Top with tomato slices, overlapping if necessary. Press gently to compact; set aside while you prepare batter.

4 In a large bowl, stir together flour, the ⅓ cup (45 g) cornmeal, sugar, baking powder, oregano, and salt. In a small bowl, combine milk, the 2 tablespoons (30 ml) olive oil, 2 tablespoons (30 ml) water, and egg whites; beat until blended. Add egg mixture to flour mixture and stir just until dry ingredients are evenly moistened.

5 Working quickly, spoon batter over tomatoes, spreading to smooth top. Bake in a 375°F (190°C) oven until topping is lightly browned and firm to the touch (about 35 minutes). Makes 6 servings.

Per serving: 392 calories (25% calories from fat), 11 g total fat, 3 g saturated fat, 15 mg cholesterol, 645 mg sodium, 54 g carbohydrates, 3 g fiber, 18 g protein, 308 mg calcium, 5 mg iron

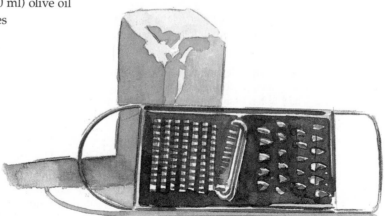

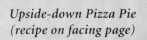
Upside-down Pizza Pie
(recipe on facing page)

Shrimp Custard

Preparation time: *15 minutes*
Cooking time: *About 30 minutes*

8 ounces (230 g) small cooked shrimp
1 cup (240 ml) nonfat milk
1 large egg
2 large egg whites
4 teaspoons (20 ml) dry sherry
2 teaspoons *each* finely chopped fresh ginger and reduced-sodium soy sauce
1 clove garlic, minced or pressed
⅛ teaspoon Oriental sesame oil
⅛ teaspoon ground white pepper
1 teaspoon sesame seeds

Divide half the shrimp evenly among four ¾-cup (180-ml) custard cups or ovenproof bowls; cover and refrigerate remaining shrimp. Set custard cups in a large baking pan at least 2 inches (5 cm) deep. In a medium-size bowl, combine milk, egg, egg whites, sherry, ginger, soy sauce, garlic, oil, and white pepper; beat lightly just until blended. Pour egg mixture evenly over shrimp in custard cups.

Set pan on center rack of a 325°F (165°C) oven. Pour boiling water into pan around cups up to level of custard. Bake until custard jiggles only slightly in center when cups are gently shaken (about 25 minutes). Lift cups from pan. Let stand for about 5 minutes before serving. Or, if made ahead, let cool; then cover and refrigerate until next day and serve cold.

Meanwhile, toast sesame seeds in a small frying pan over medium heat, stirring often, until golden (about 3 minutes). Remove from

Almost Vegetarian Egg & Cheese Dishes

✳

pan and set aside. Just before serving, top custards with remaining shrimp; then sprinkle with sesame seeds. Makes 4 servings.

Per serving: 120 calories (20% calories from fat), 2 g total fat, 1 g saturated fat, 165 mg cholesterol, 303 mg sodium, 4 g carbohydrates, 0 g fiber, 18 g protein, 115 mg calcium, 2 mg iron

✳

Eggs Benedict

Preparation time: *25 minutes*
Cooking time: *About 20 minutes*

¼ cup (60 ml) lemon juice
3 tablespoons cornstarch
1½ cups (360 ml) vegetable broth
1 cup (240 ml) low-fat (2%) milk
1 tablespoon butter or margarine, cut into chunks
2 teaspoons finely chopped fresh thyme or ½ teaspoon dried thyme
1 teaspoon *each* Dijon mustard and honey
⅛ teaspoon ground white pepper
8 very thin slices Canadian bacon (about 4 oz./115 g *total*)
4 English muffins, split
3 tablespoons (45 ml) distilled white vinegar
8 large eggs
Thyme sprigs and lemon wedges

In a small bowl, smoothly blend lemon juice and cornstarch; set aside.

In a 2- to 3-quart (1.9- to 2.8-liter) pan, combine broth, milk, butter,

chopped thyme, mustard, honey, and white pepper. Set pan over medium-high heat and, stirring with a wire whisk, slowly add cornstarch mixture. Cook, whisking constantly, until sauce comes to a boil and thickens slightly. Remove from heat and keep warm; stir occasionally.

Cook bacon in a wide nonstick frying pan over medium heat, turning as needed, just until hot and tinged with brown. Meanwhile, toast muffin halves. Arrange 2 muffin halves, cut side up, on each of 4 individual rimmed plates. Top each muffin half with a slice of bacon; set aside.

In a 5- to 6-quart (5- to 6-liter) pan, bring vinegar and 3 quarts (2.8 liters) water to a gentle boil over high heat. Reduce heat, maintaining a temperature that causes bubbles to form on pan bottom (a bubble may pop up to the top occasionally).

Cook eggs 4 at a time. To cook, hold each egg as close to water as possible; then carefully break directly into water. Cook until eggs are done to your liking; lift one egg from pan with a slotted spoon and cut into it to test (about 4 minutes for soft yolks and firm whites). Lift out cooked eggs, drain well, and keep hot until all eggs have been cooked.

To serve, arrange hot eggs on bacon-topped muffins; ladle about ½ cup (120 ml) warm sauce over each serving. Garnish with thyme sprigs and lemon wedges; serve immediately. Makes 4 servings.

Per serving: 554 calories (30% calories from fat), 18 g total fat, 7 g saturated fat, 452 mg cholesterol, 1,522 mg sodium, 65 g carbohydrates, 2 g fiber, 29 g protein, 330 mg calcium, 5 mg iron

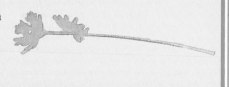

Chicken Frittata

Preparation time: *20 minutes*
Cooking time: *About 30 minutes*

2 large eggs

4 large egg whites

1 tablespoon cornstarch blended with 2 tablespoons (30 ml) cold water

1 pound (455 g) small red thin-skinned potatoes, scrubbed and thinly sliced

1 large onion, thinly sliced

1 tablespoon butter or margarine

1½ teaspoons chopped fresh rosemary or ¾ teaspoon dried rosemary, crumbled

⅓ cup (80 ml) marsala or port

1 jar (about 2 oz./55 g) diced pimentos

8 ounces (230 g) boneless, skinless chicken breast, cut into ½- by 2-inch (1- by 5-cm) strips

2 cloves garlic, minced or pressed

½ cup (55 g) shredded reduced-fat sharp Cheddar cheese

Rosemary sprigs

In a small bowl, whisk eggs, egg whites, and cornstarch mixture until blended; set aside.

In a wide nonstick frying pan with an ovenproof handle, combine potatoes, onion, and 2 teaspoons of the butter. Add ¾ cup (180 ml) water. Cover and cook over medium-high heat, stirring occasionally, until potatoes are tender when pierced (10 to 15 minutes); add more water, ¼ cup (60 ml) at a time, if pan appears dry.

Uncover pan and add chopped rosemary, marsala, and pimentos. Bring to a boil; then boil, stirring, until almost all liquid has evaporated (about 4 minutes).

Whisk egg mixture and pour over

potato mixture. Reduce heat to low and cook until eggs begin to set at pan rim (about 5 minutes). Then broil about 6 inches below heat until top of egg mixture feels set when lightly touched (about 5 minutes).

Meanwhile, melt remaining 1 teaspoon butter in a small nonstick frying pan over medium-high heat. Add chicken and garlic. Cook, stirring often, just until chicken is no longer pink in center; cut to test (3 to 4 minutes).

With a slotted spoon, lift chicken from pan and arrange over frittata. Sprinkle with cheese; broil until cheese is melted (about 30 seconds). Serve hot or warm. To serve, garnish with rosemary sprigs; then spoon from pan. Makes 4 servings.

Per serving: 339 calories (26% calories from fat), 9 g total fat, 4 g saturated fat, 157 mg cholesterol, 277 mg sodium, 31 g carbohydrates, 3 g fiber, 27 g protein, 166 mg calcium, 2 mg iron

North Beach Bruschetta

Preparation time: *20 minutes*
Cooking time: *About 7 minutes*

⅔ cup (150 g) nonfat ricotta cheese

¼ cup (25 g) shredded carrot

¼ cup (35 g) dried currants or raisins

2 tablespoons thinly sliced green onion

1 tablespoon Dijon mustard

½ teaspoon dried basil

8 ounces (230 g) unsliced crusty bread, such as Italian ciabatta or French bread

4 ounces (115 g) very thinly sliced pastrami

⅓ cup (40 g) shredded part-skim mozzarella cheese

In a medium-size bowl, stir together ricotta cheese, carrot, currants, onion, mustard, and basil. Set aside.

Cut bread in half horizontally. Set halves crust side down; if needed, cut a thin slice from cut side of halves to make each piece about 1 inch (2.5 cm) thick. Trim crust side of each piece so bread sits steadily. Then cut each piece in half crosswise.

Spread cut sides of bread with ricotta mixture. Loosely pleat pastrami over ricotta mixture, covering bread. Sprinkle with mozzarella cheese. Arrange bread on a 12- by 15-inch (30- by 38-cm) baking sheet and bake in a 400°F (205°C) oven until mozzarella cheese is melted (about 7 minutes). Makes 4 servings.

Per serving: 271 calories (12% calories from fat), 3 g total fat, 1 g saturated fat, 15 mg cholesterol, 880 mg sodium, 38 g carbohydrates, 3 g fiber, 19 g protein, 345 mg calcium, 3 mg iron

Indian-spiced Scrambled Eggs
(recipe on facing page)

Indian-spiced Scrambled Eggs *(Pictured on facing page)*

1 teaspoon olive oil

1 small onion, chopped

2 cloves garlic, minced or pressed

3 large pear-shaped (Roma-type) tomatoes (about 12 oz./340 g *total*), chopped

1½ teaspoons chili powder

½ teaspoon ground turmeric

3 tablespoons chopped cilantro

4 large eggs

8 large egg whites

2 teaspoons butter or margarine

4 pita breads (*each* about 5 inches/12.5 cm in diameter), cut crosswise into halves

Stuffed with scrambled eggs and a spicy tomato sauce, these pita bread sandwiches make a satisfying brunch or lunch.

Preparation time: 20 minutes   **Cooking time:** About 20 minutes

1 Heat oil in a wide nonstick frying pan over medium-high heat. Add onion and garlic; cook, stirring, until onion is soft (about 5 minutes). Add tomatoes, chili powder, turmeric, and 1 tablespoon of the cilantro; cook, stirring occasionally, until almost all liquid has evaporated (about 8 minutes). Transfer sauce to a bowl and keep warm. Wash and dry pan.

2 In a large bowl, beat eggs, egg whites, and ¼ cup (60 ml) water until blended. Melt butter in frying pan over medium-low heat. Add eggs and cook until softly set, gently lifting cooked portion with a wide spatula to allow uncooked eggs to flow underneath. Fill pita bread halves equally with eggs; top with sauce and remaining 2 tablespoons cilantro. Makes 4 servings.

Per serving: *335 calories (25% calories from fat), 9 g total fat, 3 g saturated fat, 218 mg cholesterol, 532 mg sodium, 42 g carbohydrates, 3 g fiber, 20 g protein, 97 mg calcium, 3 mg iron*

Chile-Cheese French Toast with Cherry Tomato Salsa

French Toast:

1 large egg

4 large egg whites

1 cup (240 ml) nonfat milk

8 diagonal slices French bread (*each* about 3 by 6 inches/ 8 by 15 cm and about ⅓ inch/ 1 cm thick)

1 cup (about 4 oz./115 g) shredded reduced-fat jack cheese

1 can (about 4 oz./115 g) diced green chiles

¼ cup (10 g) finely chopped cilantro

Cherry Tomato Salsa:

2 cups (285 g) red cherry tomatoes, cut into halves

⅓ cup (15 g) cilantro leaves

2 small fresh jalapeño chiles, seeded

1 clove garlic, peeled

2 tablespoons (30 ml) lime juice

2 tablespoons thinly sliced green onion

French toast needn't be limited to breakfast time, nor must it be sweet. This version—batter-dipped sandwiches filled with chiles and cheese—is a savory supper or lunch entrée. To save fat, we've made the batter with extra egg whites, then oven-baked the toast rather than frying it in butter.

Preparation time: 20 minutes   **Cooking time:** About 25 minutes

1 In a large bowl, beat egg, egg whites, and milk until well blended. Dip 4 slices of bread into egg mixture; turn to saturate both sides. Arrange slices in a shallow 10- by 15-inch (25- by 38-cm) nonstick baking pan.

2 Top bread in baking pan evenly with cheese, green chiles, and chopped cilantro. Dip remaining 4 bread slices into egg mixture, turning to coat both sides; place atop cheese-covered bread to form 4 sandwiches. Bake sandwiches in a 400°F (205°C) oven until bread begins to brown (about 12 minutes). Then carefully turn sandwiches over with a wide spatula; continue to bake until golden brown (about 10 more minutes).

3 Meanwhile, in a food processor, combine tomatoes, cilantro leaves, jalapeño chiles, and garlic; whirl just until tomatoes are coarsely chopped (or chop ingredients with a knife). Spoon mixture into a small bowl. Add lime juice and onion; stir to mix well.

4 To serve, transfer French toast sandwiches to individual plates. Offer salsa to add to taste. Makes 4 servings.

Per serving: *306 calories (24% calories from fat), 8 g total fat, 4 g saturated fat, 74 mg cholesterol, 811 mg sodium, 37 g carbohydrates, 3 g fiber, 22 g protein, 385 mg calcium, 2 mg iron*

Spinach Soufflé

Soufflé:

About 1 teaspoon salad oil

4½ teaspoons cornstarch

1 cup (240 ml) nonfat milk

3 tablespoons chopped fresh marjoram or 1 tablespoon dried marjoram

1 tablespoon instant minced onion

½ teaspoon pepper

⅛ teaspoon ground nutmeg

½ cup (100 g) thawed, very well drained frozen chopped spinach

¼ cup (20 g) shredded Parmesan cheese

2 large egg yolks

6 large egg whites

¼ teaspoon cream of tartar

Sour Cream Sauce:

1 cup (240 ml) nonfat sour cream

1 teaspoon sugar

⅛ teaspoon ground nutmeg

Though light and airy in texture, typical soufflés are rich in butter and eggs. With a few modifications, however, you can still enjoy these luxurious dishes—and feel virtuous while doing so! To trim down our spinach soufflé, we cut back on the egg yolks and butter and used cornstarch to thicken the mixture.

Preparation time: 20 minutes   **Cooking time:** About 30 minutes

1 Lightly coat bottom and sides of a 1½- to 1¾-quart (1.4- to 1.5-liter) soufflé dish or other straight-sided baking dish with oil.

2 Place cornstarch in a 2- to 3-quart (1.9- to 2.8-liter) pan; smoothly stir in milk. Add marjoram, onion, pepper, and nutmeg. Bring to a boil over medium-high heat, stirring. Pour mixture into a blender; add spinach and whirl until smoothly puréed. Add 2 tablespoons of the cheese and the egg yolks; whirl again until smoothly puréed.

3 In a large bowl, beat egg whites and cream of tartar with an electric mixer on high speed until whites hold soft peaks. Gently fold spinach mixture into whites; then scrape mixture into oiled dish. Sprinkle with remaining 2 tablespoons cheese. With the tip of a knife, draw a circle on top of soufflé about 1 inch (2.5 cm) in from edge of dish. Bake in a 375°F (190°C) oven until soufflé is richly browned and center jiggles only slightly when dish is gently shaken (about 25 minutes).

4 Meanwhile, in a small bowl, beat sour cream, sugar, and nutmeg until smoothly blended. Set aside.

5 Serve soufflé immediately; offer sour cream sauce to add to taste. Makes 4 servings.

Per serving: *180 calories (29% calories from fat), 5 g total fat, 2 g saturated fat, 111 mg cholesterol, 281 mg sodium, 14 g carbohydrates, 1 g fiber, 16 g protein, 291 mg calcium, 2 mg iron*

Scrambled Eggs & Bulgur

2 cups (470 ml) vegetable broth

1 cup (175 g) bulgur

2 teaspoons butter or margarine

1 medium-size onion, thinly sliced

1 medium-size red bell pepper (about 6 oz./170 g), seeded and thinly sliced

2 large eggs

4 large egg whites

¼ cup (20 g) grated Parmesan cheese

Serve this hearty entrée as you would any other egg dish, at brunch or for a light lunch or dinner.

Preparation time: 10 minutes, plus 10 minutes for bulgur to stand **Cooking time:** About 15 minutes

1 In a 1- to 1½-quart (950-ml to 1.4-liter) pan, bring broth to a boil over high heat. Stir in bulgur; cover, remove from heat, and let stand until liquid has been absorbed (about 10 minutes).

2 Meanwhile, melt 1 teaspoon of the butter in a wide nonstick frying pan over medium heat. Add onion and bell pepper; cook, stirring often, until onion is lightly browned (about 10 minutes). Add water, 1 tablespoon (15 ml) at a time, if pan appears dry. Meanwhile, in a small bowl, beat eggs, egg whites, and ¼ cup (60 ml) water until blended.

3 Add remaining 1 teaspoon butter to onion mixture in pan and reduce heat to medium-low. Add egg mixture; cook until eggs are softly set, gently lifting cooked portion with a wide spatula to allow uncooked eggs to flow underneath.

4 Divide bulgur and egg mixture equally among 4 individual plates. Sprinkle with cheese. Makes 4 servings.

Per serving: *254 calories (25% calories from fat), 7 g total fat, 3 g saturated fat, 116 mg cholesterol, 726 mg sodium, 35 g carbohydrates, 8 g fiber, 14 g protein, 123 mg calcium, 2 mg iron*

Squash Strata with Cranberry Chutney *(Pictured on page 94)*

Squash Strata:

1 large onion, very thinly sliced
1½ cups (268 g) canned pumpkin
2 large eggs
4 large egg whites
¾ cup (180 ml) half-and-half
½ cup (120 ml) nonfat milk
1 tablespoon cornstarch
1½ teaspoons chopped fresh thyme or ½ teaspoon dried thyme
1 cup (about 3 oz./85 g) grated Parmesan cheese
9 slices egg sandwich bread or whole wheat sandwich bread, torn into large pieces

Cranberry Chutney:

½ cup (120 ml) currant or raspberry jelly
½ cup (120 ml) orange marmalade
1 cup (95 g) fresh cranberries
¼ cup (23 g) dried cranberries or raisins
1 teaspoon balsamic vinegar (or to taste)

Garnish:

1 to 2 tablespoons finely chopped parsley

Deep orange pumpkin contributes flavor and color to this tempting layered casserole. While the dish bakes, you can easily prepare a sweet-tart chutney made with both fresh and dried cranberries to serve alongside.

Preparation time: 25 minutes **Cooking time:** About 1 hour and 20 minutes

1 In a wide nonstick frying pan, combine onion and 2 tablespoons (30 ml) water. Cook over medium-high heat, stirring often, until liquid evaporates and browned bits stick to pan bottom (about 10 minutes). To deglaze pan, add ¼ cup (60 ml) more water, stirring to loosen browned bits from pan. Continue to cook until onion is lightly browned (about 10 more minutes); add water, 1 tablespoon (15 ml) at a time, if pan appears dry. Remove onion from pan and set aside.

2 In a food processor or a large bowl, combine pumpkin, eggs, egg whites, half-and-half, milk, cornstarch, and thyme. Whirl or beat with an electric mixer until smoothly puréed. Stir in three-fourths of the cheese; set aside.

3 Arrange 3 slices of bread (overlapping, if necessary) over bottom of a greased deep 2½- to 3-quart (2.4- to 2.8-liter) casserole. Top evenly with a third each of the onion and pumpkin mixture. Repeat layers twice, ending with pumpkin mixture. Sprinkle with remaining cheese.

4 Cover tightly and bake in a 350°F (175°C) oven for 30 minutes. Then uncover and continue to bake until top is tinged with brown and a knife inserted in center comes out clean (about 30 more minutes).

5 Meanwhile, in a 1½- to 2-quart (1.4- to 1.9-liter) pan, combine ¼ cup (60 ml) water, jelly, marmalade, fresh cranberries, and dried cranberries. Bring to a boil over medium-high heat, stirring. Reduce heat and boil gently, stirring occasionally, until fresh cranberries split and are soft (about 8 minutes). Remove from heat and stir in vinegar; set aside.

6 Let casserole cool for about 5 minutes before serving. Garnish with parsley. Offer chutney to spoon over individual servings. Makes 6 servings.

Per serving: *462 calories (22% calories from fat), 12 g total fat, 6 g saturated fat, 93 mg cholesterol, 586 mg sodium, 75 g carbohydrates, 4 g fiber, 16 g protein, 336 mg calcium, 3 mg iron*

Corn Custard *(Pictured on facing page)*

4 teaspoons yellow cornmeal

1 can (about 15 oz./425 g) cream-style corn

½ cup (120 ml) nonfat milk

¼ cup (60 ml) half-and-half

2 teaspoons cornstarch

¼ teaspoon salt

⅛ teaspoon ground white pepper

2 large eggs

2 large egg whites

1 package (about 10 oz./285 g) frozen corn kernels, thawed and drained

1 jar (about 2 oz./55 g) diced pimentos

Italian parsley sprigs

Despite its lush flavor and texture, this silky custard is pleasingly lean. To achieve velvety richness without fat, we use a combination of nonfat milk, half-and-half, and puréed cream-style corn in place of the typical butter and cream.

Preparation time: 10 minutes   **Cooking time:** About 1½ hours

1 Sprinkle cornmeal over bottom of four 1¼-cup (300-ml) custard cups or oven-proof bowls, using 1 teaspoon of the cornmeal for each cup. Set cups in a large baking pan at least 2 inches (5 cm) deep.

2 In a food processor or blender, combine cream-style corn, milk, half-and-half, cornstarch, salt, white pepper, eggs, and egg whites. Whirl until smooth; stir in corn kernels and pimentos. Working quickly, divide mixture evenly among cups.

3 Set pan on center rack of a 325°F (165°C) oven. Pour boiling water into pan around cups up to level of custard. Bake until custard jiggles only slightly in center when cups are gently shaken (about 1½ hours). Lift cups from pan. Let stand for 5 minutes before serving. Garnish with parsley sprigs. Makes 4 servings.

Per serving: *235 calories (19% calories from fat), 5 g total fat, 2 g saturated fat, 112 mg cholesterol, 524 mg sodium, 41 g carbohydrates, 3 g fiber, 11 g protein, 77 mg calcium, 1 mg iron*

Overnight Fiery Oven Strata

Oven Strata:

12 slices firm-textured whole wheat sandwich bread

2 cups (140 g) thinly sliced mushrooms

1 cup (100 g) sliced green onions

1 large can (about 7 oz./200 g) diced green chiles

3 cups (about 12 oz./340 g) shredded reduced-fat sharp Cheddar cheese

3 large eggs

4 large egg whites

2½ cups (590 ml) nonfat milk

1 tablespoon dry mustard

About 1 teaspoon liquid hot pepper seasoning (or to taste)

1 cup (115 g) coarsely crushed low-fat baked tortilla chips

Salsa:

2 medium-size tomatoes (about 12 oz./340 g *total*), chopped

½ small onion, finely chopped

1 can (about 4 oz./115 g) diced green chiles

4 teaspoons (20 ml) distilled white vinegar

1 tablespoon chopped cilantro

Sugar

This version of the familiar oven strata—a layered make-ahead casserole of bread, cheese, and eggs—gets a fiery kick from chiles and hot pepper seasoning. Serve it with a homemade tomato salsa.

Preparation time: 20 minutes, plus at least 8 hours to chill   **Cooking time:** About 55 minutes

1 Line bottom of a 9- by 13-inch (23- by 33-cm) baking pan with a single layer of bread; use about half the bread slices, trimming them to fit and reserving scraps. Top bread with half each of the mushrooms and green onions, half the large can of chiles, and half the cheese. Repeat layers, starting with remaining bread (and any reserved scraps) and ending with cheese.

2 In a large bowl, beat eggs and egg whites until blended. Add milk, mustard, and hot pepper seasoning; beat to blend well. Pour egg mixture slowly over ingredients in pan; cover and refrigerate for at least 8 hours or up to 24 hours. Then uncover, sprinkle with tortilla chips, and bake in a 350°F (175°C) oven until golden (about 55 minutes). Let stand for about 15 minutes before serving.

3 Meanwhile, in a medium-size bowl, stir together tomatoes, chopped onion, the 4-ounce (115-g) can of chiles, vinegar, and cilantro. Season to taste with sugar.

4 To serve, cut strata into squares or spoon it from pan. Offer salsa to add to taste. Makes 10 servings.

Per serving: *297 calories (29% calories from fat), 10 g total fat, 5 g saturated fat, 89 mg cholesterol, 759 mg sodium, 32 g carbohydrates, 5 g fiber, 22 g protein, 439 mg calcium, 2 mg iron*

Corn Custard
(recipe on facing page)

Spoonbread with Berries

Preparation time: *About 20 minutes*
Cooking time: *About 1 hour*

10	cups (1.4 kg) mixed fresh berries, such as blackberries, raspberries, and hulled strawberries
⅓	cup (70 g) sugar
4	cups (950 ml) low-fat (1%) milk
¼	cup (55 g) butter or margarine
2	tablespoons sugar
½	teaspoon salt
1⅓	cups (185 g) yellow cornmeal
6	large eggs, separated
4	teaspoons baking powder
1	teaspoon cream of tartar
2	cups (470 ml) lemon-flavored nonfat yogurt

In a large bowl, combine berries and the ⅓ cup (70 g) sugar. Mix gently; then set aside.

In a 5- to 6-quart (5- to 6-liter) pan, combine milk, butter, the 2 tablespoons sugar, and salt. Heat over medium-low heat, stirring occasionally, until mixture is just steaming (about 4 minutes). Reduce heat to low and gradually add cornmeal, stirring constantly; cook, stirring, until mixture is thick (about 6 minutes). Remove from heat and let cool slightly. Whisk in egg yolks and baking powder until blended; set aside.

In a large bowl, beat egg whites and cream of tartar with an electric mixer on high speed until whites hold stiff peaks. Blend 1 cup (240 ml) of the beaten egg whites into cornmeal mixture; then gently fold cornmeal mixture into remaining whites. Scrape mixture into a buttered 9- by 13-inch (23- by 33-cm)

Breakfasts
✳

baking pan. Bake in a 350°F (175°C) oven until top of spoonbread is golden brown and firm to the touch and a wooden pick inserted in center comes out clean (about 45 minutes).

Meanwhile, in a medium-size bowl, mix yogurt with 2 cups (290 g) of the sugared berries.

Top portions of spoonbread with berry-yogurt mixture; serve remaining berries and their juices alongside. Makes 8 servings.

Per serving: 415 calories (25% calories from fat), 12 g total fat, 6 g saturated fat, 180 mg cholesterol, 577 mg sodium, 65 g carbohydrates, 8 g fiber, 14 g protein, 446 mg calcium, 3 mg iron

Quick Cinnamon Buns

Preparation time: *35 minutes*
Cooking time: *About 30 minutes*

Filling:

½	cup (75 g) raisins
¾	cup (165 g) firmly packed brown sugar
4	ounces (115 g) Neufchâtel cheese, at room temperature
⅓	cup (28 g) graham cracker crumbs
1½	teaspoons ground cinnamon

Buns:

2	cups (250 g) bread flour or all-purpose flour
1	tablespoon baking powder
¼	teaspoon salt
¾	cup (180 ml) low-fat (2%) cottage cheese
⅓	cup (70 g) granulated sugar
⅓	cup (80 ml) nonfat milk
¼	cup (60 ml) salad oil
2	teaspoons vanilla

Glaze:

1	cup (120 g) sifted powdered sugar
¼	to ½ teaspoon vanilla

In a small bowl, combine raisins and ½ cup (120 ml) hot water; let stand until raisins are softened (about 10 minutes), stirring occasionally. In another small bowl, mix brown sugar, Neufchâtel cheese, graham cracker crumbs, and cinnamon until mixture resembles coarse, moist crumbs; set aside.

In a medium-size bowl, combine flour, baking powder, and salt; set aside.

In a food processor or a large bowl, combine cottage cheese, granulated sugar, milk, oil, and the 2 teaspoons vanilla. Whirl or beat with an electric mixer until smoothly puréed. Add flour mixture; whirl or stir to make a soft dough. Transfer dough to a lightly floured board and knead several times, or until dough holds together.

With floured fingers, pat dough into a 9- by 14-inch (23- by 35.5-cm) rectangle. Distribute brown sugar mixture evenly over dough to within ½ inch (1 cm) of edge; press mixture gently into dough. Drain raisins well; scatter over sugar mixture and press gently into dough.

With floured fingers, snugly roll up dough jelly-roll style, starting with a long edge; pinch ends and seam to seal. Using a serrated knife, cut roll into 12 equal slices; if desired, wipe knife clean between cuts. Place buns, cut side up, in a greased nonstick or regular 10-inch (25-cm) cheesecake pan with a removable rim. Bake in a 400°F (205°C) oven until buns are richly browned (about 30 minutes).

Meanwhile, in a small bowl, beat powdered sugar, about 1 tablespoon (15 ml) water, and the ¼ to ½ teaspoon vanilla until smoothly blended. If needed, add more water, ½ teaspoon at a time, to make glaze thin enough to drizzle. Set glaze aside.

Remove baked buns from oven and let cool on a rack for 5 minutes. Carefully remove pan rim; stir glaze and drizzle over buns. Serve at once. Makes 12 buns.

Per bun: 301 calories (23% calories from fat), 8 g total fat, 2 g saturated fat, 8 mg cholesterol, 292 mg sodium, 52 g carbohydrates, 1 g fiber, 6 g protein, 114 mg calcium, 2 mg iron

Cheese Blintzes

Preparation time: *30 minutes*
Cooking time: *About 25 minutes*

2	large eggs
½	cup (60 g) all-purpose flour
¾	cup (180 ml) nonfat milk
	About 3 tablespoons butter or margarine
12	ounces (340 g) farmer's cheese or dry-curd cottage cheese
2	to 3 tablespoons sugar
1	tablespoon (15 ml) plain nonfat yogurt or nonfat milk
2	teaspoons grated lemon peel
¾	teaspoon vanilla
½	teaspoon ground cinnamon
	Finely shredded lemon peel (optional)
¾	cup (180 ml) strawberry preserves
¾	cup (180 ml) nonfat sour cream

In a blender or a medium-size bowl, combine eggs, flour, and milk. Whirl or beat until smoothly blended.

Melt ½ teaspoon of the butter in a small nonstick frying pan over medium heat. Pour about 2 tablespoons (30 ml) of the batter into hot pan; tip and swirl pan to cover bottom evenly with batter. Cook until top of pancake feels dry when lightly touched (about 1 minute). Gently turn pancake over with a wide spatula (be careful not to tear pancake); cook until faintly speckled with brown on bottom. Turn pancake out of pan and lay flat.

Repeat to cook remaining pancakes,

stirring batter before you make each pancake and adding more butter to pan as needed. Stack pancakes, separating them with wax paper or plastic wrap; you should have about 12 pancakes.

In a food processor or a large bowl, combine farmer's cheese, sugar, yogurt, grated lemon peel, vanilla, and cinnamon; whirl or beat with an electric mixer until well blended.

Divide filling into as many portions as you have pancakes. Lay one pancake flat, darker side down. Mound one portion of filling in center. Fold opposite sides of pancake over filling; then fold ends over filling to enclose. Set blintz seam side down and pat gently to make filling evenly thick. Repeat to fill remaining pancakes. (At this point, you may arrange blintzes in a 12- by 15-inch/30- by 38-cm pan, cover tightly, and refrigerate for up to 4 hours.)

Melt 2 teaspoons of the butter in a wide nonstick frying pan over medium-high heat. Add about half the blintzes (do not crowd pan); cook until blintzes are golden brown on bottom (about 1 minute). Turn with a wide spatula and cook until browned on other side (1 to 2 more minutes). Repeat to cook remaining blintzes; as blintzes are cooked, transfer them to a platter and keep warm. Garnish with shredded lemon peel, if desired. Offer preserves and sour cream to add to taste. Makes 4 servings.

Per serving: 521 calories (29% calories from fat), 18 g total fat, 4 g saturated fat, 153 mg cholesterol, 446 mg sodium, 75 g carbohydrates, 1 g fiber, 22 g protein, 247 mg calcium, 2 mg iron

Squash Strata with Cranberry Chutney
(recipe on page 89)

Index